IRON CONDOR

CONDOR

NEUTRAL STRATEGY FOR UNCOMMON PROFIT

ERNIE ZERENNER & MICHAEL PHILLIPS

Marketplace Books
Glenelg, Maryland

Publisher: Chris Myers
VP/General Manager: John Boyer
Executive Editor: Jody Costa
Development Editor: Courtney Jenkins
Art Director: Larry Strauss
Graphic Designer: Jennifer Marin
Production Designer: Jessica Weedlun

ISBN: 1-59280-392-X
ISBN 13: 978-1-59280-392-7

Printed in the United States of America.

TABLE OF CONTENTS

FOREWORD

WHY YOU HAVE TO READ THIS BOOK!

This is your complete A to Z guide for trading iron condors, a neutral stock options strategy. An iron condor strategy takes advantage of the stock market's primary activity, which is basically not doing anything but making slight deviations in price from the previous day, week, month, and year. Iron condors perform best when the stock market is stagnant, which enables users to generate income when other strategies underperform. This is not a book for those interested in trading options as a speculative investment vehicle.

The concepts, ideas, rules of thumb, and real-world examples presented in the text have been gleaned from the PowerOptionsApplied newsletter's successful trading of the strategy over the last five years (www.poweroptionsapplied.com).

Other option books explain the theory and concepts of trading the iron condor, but this text goes further by presenting real-world examples, real-world profits, and real-world mistakes. This book presents the concept of optimally trading iron condors, balancing risk, reward, volatility, stop-losses, and other parameters to achieve the best results from trading the strategy.

For illustrative purposes, graphics from the PowerOptions web site (www.poweropt.com) are used throughout. The PowerOptions web site provides powerful and useful tools for not only finding and managing iron condors, but other stock options strategies as well, such as covered calls, naked puts, etc.

The real power needed for investing with options comes from knowledge and experience. This book will go a long way toward supplying the knowledge necessary for investing with iron condors.

The authors would like to thank Michael Chupka for his tireless efforts in reviewing this book.

For additional information regarding this book please refer to: www.PowerOptionsApplied.com/additional.asp.

Chapter 1

INTRODUCTION

Technological and structural advances in trading markets have given investors a plethora of choices for managing portfolios, and especially for administrating portfolios using equity options. In this book, we will examine one of the many choices available to investors: *the iron condor stock options strategy.*

This book will aid investors in making a profit and in managing the risk associated with the iron condor strategy. Readers will learn the advantages and pitfalls of trading iron condors through the real-world trading experiences and practical rule of thumb recommendations presented. Methods and strategies for reducing and managing the risk of iron condors will be illustrated in order to increase investors' potential for success with the strategy. Readers will learn how to: search for, find, analyze, enter, manage, roll, and exit iron condor investments. Additionally, readers will be introduced to optimizing the strategy for maximized returns.

"There's always a bull market somewhere," is a common expression parlayed in stock investing. A similar expression could be made for stock option investing: "There's always a good stock option strategy." Hence, there are market conditions in which an iron condor is an appropriate strategy for implementation and market conditions in which the strategy should be avoided. An iron condor is a neutral stock option strategy and its best performance is observed during periods of relatively small market movements. Market movements of less than plus or minus 5% in a month are generally acceptable for trading the strategy. Iron condors are best avoided during instances of large market movements.

The prevailing mantra of financial gurus for the buy-and-hold stock strategy is to invest with a diversified portfolio. The idea behind diversification is to invest in numerous stocks so a large loss suffered for one position translates into only a small loss for the aggregate portfolio. Similarly, diversification in option investing should also be considered a prudent choice. An investor should not consider investing a majority of capital with iron condor positions. A sudden large market movement occurring as a result of an event such as the 9/11 tragedy, Hurricane Katrina, or the Lehman Brothers bankruptcy could result in a significant loss. In general, the iron condor strategy is a profitable and uneventful strategy; however, it occasionally can become very risky and has the potential for causing large losses.

Any investor should be able to trade iron condors with approval from their broker and a diversified portfolio. Investors not capable of trading this strategy in a diversified manner should forgo it. Beginner investors should limit their exposure to iron condors to less than 10 percent of their portfolio, while more experienced investors can increase their exposure to maybe 25 percent. All investors new to trading iron condors should consider back testing and/or paper trading the positions for at least a couple of months before attempting to trade the strategy with their precious capital. Back testing enables investors to gain experience more quickly than paper trading.

Additionally, back testing provides investors the capability to attempt many different scenarios in order to find the optimal approach for a strategy. PowerOptions (www.poweropt.com) provides back testing capability for those seeking to quickly learn how to trade a strategy.

The iron condor strategy generally performs best in markets with heightened volatility as a result of a past market-moving event and with the anticipation that volatility levels will return to normal. Conversely, the strategy is the most dangerous and the most difficult to implement during periods of very low market volatility. During low market volatility, a major market event can cause market volatility to significantly increase, and the iron condor positions can then morph from profit-making machines to potential loss quagmires.

The stock market has a tendency to trade sideways or remain in a trading range for large periods of time. The buy-and-hold stock strategy does not perform well in stagnant markets. However, the iron condor is well-suited for generating returns in a market environment that is mildly volatile, i.e., movements less than plus or minus 5 percent per month, and stuck in a trading range.

A significant amount of stock option literature tends to focus heavily on the Greeks; Delta, Gamma, Vega, Theta, etc. The Greek-related material proffered by many financial authors sounds sophisticated and intelligent, but in reality, an average reader is often left confused and bewildered by the material presented. In this book, discussions related to the "Greeks" will be avoided in order to offer practical information that any reader can understand.

STOCK OPTION BASICS

Before we delve into the mechanics of the iron condor, we must cover some basic information related to stock options.

Options Definition

Options are contracts giving purchasers the right, but not the obligation, to buy or sell shares of stock. Option sellers are obligated to deliver or accept stock as required by the specifications of the option contract. Investors can trade these contracts just as they can buy or sell (short) shares of stock. Each option contract typically represents 100 shares of the underlying security; therefore, if an investor purchases one option contract, he or she is purchasing the right to buy or sell 100 shares of the underlying security. Five option contracts would represent 500 shares, and so on. There are two types of options available to investors: *calls* and *puts*.

Buying a call option gives the owner of the contract the right, but not the obligation, to buy shares of stock at a set price (called the *strike price*) at any time before the option expires (called the *expiration date*). Buying a put option gives the owner of the contract the right, but not the obligation, to sell (force someone to buy) shares of stock at a set strike price prior to the expiration date. These definitions apply to investors who purchase options speculating that the stock will rise or fall to make a profit. On the other side of these transactions are options sellers. Selling a call obligates the investor to deliver shares of stock at the strike price to the option buyer. Selling a put obligates the investor to buy shares of stock at the strike price.

Table 1.1: Option Rights and Obligations Chart

	Buyer	Seller
Call	Owns the right to buy shares of stock from the call seller	Obligated to deliver shares of stock to the call buyer
Put	Owns the right to sell shares of stock to the put seller	Obligated to buy shares of stock from the put buyer

But, what does that really mean? Let's break down Table 1.1 to a more basic view.

Table 1.2: Option Position and Market Sentiment

	Buyer	Seller
Call	Speculative Bullish (Long Call)	Neutral to Bearish (Naked Call)
Put	Speculative Bearish (Long Put)	Neutral to Bullish (Naked Put)

Table 1.2 illustrates the market sentiment for the four basic option transactions. These four transactions are *uncovered positions*, meaning that no shares of the underlying stock are owned or shorted with the option trade.

The call buyer has purchased the right to buy shares of stock at a set price, called the *strike price*. This is a very bullish position, as the investor needs the stock to rise in price so the value of the call option will increase in value. The investor can then *exercise* the option and purchase shares of stock at the strike price, or simply *sell to close* the option to realize a profit. This is the long call position. The profit potential for a long call strategy is essentially unlimited within the timeframe of the contract, as the stock could continue to rise indefinitely.

The put buyer has purchased the right to sell shares of stock at the strike price at any time between entry and the expiration date. This is a very bearish position, as the investor needs the stock to fall in price so the put option will increase in value. The investor can then exercise the put option and force someone to buy shares of stock, or the investor can simply sell to close the option to realize a profit. This is the long put position.

The call seller has entered into a contract that obligates him to deliver shares of stock at the option strike price. The investor collects a premium in return for providing this obligation. If the stock price remains below the strike price of the call, the option will *expire worthless* and the investor will keep the premium. This strategy is called a *naked call trade* and is a neutral to bearish position because the investor hopes the stock remains at the same price or declines in value.

This is a very risky strategy, as the potential loss is unlimited. Theoretically, the stock price could rise infinitely. If there is a large increase in the stock price, the investor may be forced to buy shares of stock at the higher price to fulfill the obligation of the option contract for delivering the stock. This could result in a significant loss. To avoid this, the call seller can *buy to close* the option contract at any time before expiration to limit the loss if the stock price goes against him. This would remove the obligation to deliver the stock.

The put seller has entered into a contract that obligates her to buy shares of stock at the option strike price. The investor will receive a premium in return for providing this obligation. If the stock price remains above the strike price, the put will expire worthless and the investor will keep the premium. This is the *naked put trade*, which is a neutral to bullish strategy and is used by investors to potentially buy shares of stock at a discount. The risk in this strategy is if the stock falls in price. The investor may be forced to buy shares of stock

Several terms have been introduced that a reader may or may not be familiar with, such as *strike price, expiration date, premium*, and *expire worthless*. In order to fully understand how options work, investors need to make sure they are very familiar with these terms. Please refer to the glossary for additional information.

at the option strike price to cover the obligation, even though the stock is trading at a much lower price; however, the investor can buy to close the put obligation at any time prior to the expiration date to limit losses if sentiment on the position has changed.

Strike Price

Each optionable stock will have several strike prices to choose from to buy or sell for both calls and puts, as illustrated in Figure 1.1. In the case of a call buyer, the strike price represents the price of the stock at which the call buyer has the right to purchase shares of stock from the call seller. If the stock price is trading above the strike price of the call, the option is *in-the-money* (ITM). The call buyer can exercise the call contract, buy shares of stock at the strike price, and then sell the shares at market for the higher value. The call seller would have to deliver shares of stock at the value of the strike price to fulfill the obligation, even though the market is offering a higher stock price. If the stock price is trading below the strike price of the call, the option is *out-of-the-money* (OTM). If the call option were OTM at expiration, the call would expire worthless. The call buyer would not exer-

Figure 1.1: Option Chain - Stock XYZ trading at $50.00		

Strike	Call Sym	Put Sym
Stock (XYZ) $50.00	Near Month Options - 30 days to expiration	
35.00	XYZGG	XYZSG Out of the Money Puts
40.00	XYZGH In the Money Calls	XYZSH (Strike Price below
Option Strike ◀━▶ 45.00	XYZGI (highlighted)	XYZSI Stock Price)
Prices 50.00	XYZGJ	XYZSJ
55.00	XYZGK Out of the Money Calls	XYZSK In the Money Puts
60.00	XYZGL (Strike price above	XYZSL (highlighted)
65.00	XYZGM Stock Price)	XYZSM

Source: PowerOptions (www.poweropt.com)

cise the right to buy shares of stock at the strike price when the stock could be purchased from the market at a lower price.

Put options have the opposite requirements of call options. A call buyer owns the right to purchase shares of stock, whereas a put buyer owns the right to sell shares of stock. A put buyer is a bearish investor, because the put will gain in value as the underlying security falls in price. For a put buyer the strike price represents the value that the investor can force the put seller to buy shares of stock. If the stock is trading below the put strike price, the put is ITM, the opposite from the call scenario. If the stock is trading below the put strike price, the put buyer can force the put seller to buy shares of stock at a higher value than the current market price. If the stock is trading above the strike price, the put option is OTM and will expire worthless. The put buyer would not exercise the right to sell shares of stock at the strike price if the shares could be sold at the market for a higher value. Table 1.3 shows the relationship between the stock price and the strike price for in-the-money and out-of-the-money call and put options.

Table 1.3: ITM / OTM Quick Chart

	In-the-Money	Out-of-the-Money
Call	Stock Price above the Strike Price	Stock Price below the Strike Price
Put	Stock Price below the Strike Price	Stock Price above the Strike Price

Expiration Date

The owner of the contract, whether it is a call or a put, has a set time frame to exercise this right before the option expires. This is known as the expiration date. Standard stock equity options expire on the third Friday of the specific expiration month. Technically, options expire on the third Saturday of the specific expiration month, but the last day investors can actively trade, close, exercise, or assign their options is the third Friday. Some index options may expire on the morning of the third Friday or the third Thursday afternoon. Recently, some indexes have released weekly options, and some ETFs (exchange traded funds) have released quarterly expiration options. This text focuses on the standard expiration, those options that expire on the third Friday of every month.

Each optionable stock will have various expiration months that the investor can choose to buy or sell. These different months are referred to as the *option series* for that stock. There are three possible expiration series for an optionable stock:

JAJO—January, April, July, and October

FMAN—February, May, August, and November

MJSD—March, June, September, and December

Regardless of the expiration series, every optionable stock will have the near month available. The example in Figure 1.2 shows the MJSD series, but since the March and April expiration dates have already passed, May is listed as the near option. On the option chain to the left, you can see that the July and August options are not yet available, but the options with those expiration dates will be released once the next expiration date passes. The July options for this stock will be released the Monday following May expiration.

At the time of this publication, 40 percent of the more than 3,000 optionable stocks, indexes, and ETFs also have LEAPS options available. LEAPS are Long-term Equity AnticiPation Securities that typically have a January expiration date one or two years out in time. Some

Figure 1.2: A Stock with MJSD Expiration Series

Strike	Call Sym.
May 16 days left	
40.00	HPEH
45.00	HPEI
50.00	HPEJ
55.00	HPEK
60.00	HPEL
65.00	HPEM
June 51 days left	
30.00	HPFF
35.00	HPFG
40.00	HPFH
45.00	HPFI
50.00	HPFJ
55.00	HPFK
60.00	HPFL
65.00	HPFM
September 142 days left	
30.00	HPIF
35.00	HPIG
40.00	HPIH
45.00	HPII
50.00	HPIJ
55.00	HPIK
60.00	HPIL
65.00	HPIM
70.00	HPIN
75.00	HPIO
December 233 days left	
40.00	HPLH
45.00	HPLI
50.00	HPLJ
55.00	HPLK
60.00	HPLL
65.00	HPLM
70.00	HPLN
75.00	HPLO

Source: PowerOptions (www.poweropt.com)

indexes and ETFs will have December or March expiration dates one or two years out in time. During the months of May through July, the near-term January LEAPS shift to regular contracts, and a new series of LEAPS one year more out in time are released.

Recently, the conversion schedule for LEAPS has been adjusted. The near-term January options still convert to regular options in the months of May, June, and July, but the new far-out LEAPS are not scheduled to be released until September, October, and November. The conversion and release dates are determined by the options expiration series. For example, those optionable stocks with LEAPS available in the January class (JAJO series) will have the near LEAPS options convert in May, and the new two-year-out LEAPS will be available to trade in September. Those optionable stocks with LEAPS available in the February class (FMAN series) will have the near LEAPS convert in June, and the new two-year-out LEAPS will be available to trade in October. For the March class (MJSD series), the near LEAPS will convert in July, and the new two-year-out LEAPS will be available to trade in November.

LEAPS options are the same as near-term options with the exceptions that the expiration date is further out in time and the option *root symbol* for a LEAPS option will be slightly different from the near-term options.

Option Symbols

On the exchange, stocks, indexes, and ETFs are identified by a specific symbol. The same is true for options, however as of the writing of this book, symbols for options are in the process of being modified and some of the following material presented will become obsolete.

Each option has its own specific symbol that identifies to which underlying security the option is related, the expiration month, the strike price for the option, and if the option is a call or a put.

Referring to Figure 1.2, we see that all of the options listed have the same first two letters: HP. The first two or three letters of an option symbol are the root letters, and they identify the underlying security for the option. These particular options are for Helmerich & Payne Inc., which trades under the symbol HP. Options for IBM, International Business Machines, have the root symbol IBM.

The next letter following the root letters of an option signifies the expiration month. In Figure 1.2, note that the third letter for each of the May options is E, for June the third letter is F, and for September the third letter is I. For IBM, the May symbols would start off as IBME, for June IBMF, and for September IBMI. The expiration month letter is always the second to last letter for the option symbol. Call options use the expiration month letters of A through L. Put options use the expiration month letters of M through Z. Table 1.4 is a quick reference chart for the expiration codes for every month for call and put options.

Table 1.4: Expiration Month Codes

	JAN	FEB	MAR	APR	MAY	JUN	JUL	AUG	SEP	OCT	NOV	DEC
Calls	A	B	C	D	E	F	G	H	I	J	K	L
Puts	M	N	O	P	Q	R	S	T	U	V	W	X

The final letter of the option symbol designates the strike price of the option. In Figure 1.2, notice how all of the 55 strike call options end in the letter K, and all of the 50 strike call options end in the letter J. The symbol for the 55 strike put for HP would also end in the letter K, just as the symbol for the 50 strike put would end in the letter J.

Since there are so many different strikes on stocks of various prices, these numbers might also indicate other strikes as well. A 150 strike option will also end in J, as typically will a 250 strike call and a 350 strike call.

You will not need to memorize these codes to be a successful options trader, but having the information close by or in the back of your mind might help you avoid any mistakes when placing a trade.

TRADING OPTIONS

Like shares of stock, option contracts are listed on the exchanges with a *bid* and *ask* price. An option buyer will pay the value of the listed ask price, while an option seller will collect a premium at the bid price. The market maker for the underlying security determines the bid and ask prices for each option. The difference between the bid price and the ask price is referred to as the *bid-ask spread*. The market maker can manipulate the market by setting the bid-ask spread wider apart. He earns money by purchasing contracts at the bid price and then selling them to the public at the ask price.

Figure 1.3: Stock XYZ at $50, 30 days to expiration								
More Info	Strike	Call Sym	Opt Bid	Opt Ask	Put Sym	Opt Bid	Opt Ask
Stock (XYZ) $50.00				Near Month Options - 30 days to expiration			
▶	35.00	XYZGG	14.70	15.10	XYZSG	0.00	0.10
▶	40.00	XYZGH	9.70	10.50	XYZSH	0.00	0.15
▶	45.00	XYZGI	5.10	Bid - Ask Spread: 5.40	XYZSI	0.25	Bid-Ask Spread: 0.40
▶	50.00	XYZGJ	1.55	1.80	XYZSJ	1.65	1.85
▶	55.00	XYZGK	0.15	0.30	XYZSK	5.20	5.50
▶	60.00	XYZGL	0.00	0.10	XYZSL	9.80	10.40
▶	65.00	XYZGM	0.00	0.10	XYZSM	14.90	15.40

Source: PowerOptions (www.poweropt.com)

The bid-ask spread prevents investors from buying large amounts of contracts and then selling them quickly, as this would cause an immediate loss on the position. Without the spread in place, it is possible that investors could manipulate volume by buying large amounts of contracts and then selling them right away without penalty.

Figure 1.3 shows the bid-ask spread for calls and puts on a given stock. For the 50 strike call, the bid price is $1.55 and the ask price is $1.80. This spread makes it impractical for any investor or group of investors to buy a large number of contracts at the ask price and then sell them immediately, as they would incur a $0.25 loss.

The bid-ask spread for the 50 strike put is slightly higher at $0.20; the bid price is $1.65 and the ask price is $1.85.

Since each contract represents 100 shares of the underlying security, the total cost to buy an option would be:

Option Ask Price * Number of Contracts * 100

In the above example, the ask price for the 50 strike call is $1.80. One contract would cost the option buyer $180 (plus commissions):

$1.80 * 1 * 100 = $180 (plus commissions)

The investor pays $1.80 for each share that is represented by the contract. If an investor purchased 5 contracts, it would cost $900; 10 contracts would cost the option investor $1,800.

For the 50 strike put, the ask price is $1.85. An investor buying one contract would pay $185, 5 contracts would cost $925, and 10 contracts would cost $1,850 (all plus commissions).

OPTION PRICING COMPONENTS

The option premium has two components, *intrinsic value* and *time value*.

Intrinsic value refers to the amount of monetary value the strike price of the option is ITM (in-the-money). As noted earlier, a call option is ITM if the stock price is trading above the strike price. For an ITM call, the intrinsic value equals the current stock price minus the strike price (if the stock price is greater than the call strike price).

The put option is ITM if the stock price is below the strike price of the option. For an ITM put option, the intrinsic value equals the strike price minus the stock price (if the stock price is less than the put strike price). Intrinsic value represents the value of the option at expiration if the price of the underlying stock remains unchanged.

Figure 1.3 shows that the 45 call option has an ask price of $5.40. If XYZ is trading at $50, the 45 strike option is 5 points ITM, or has $5 of intrinsic value. Remember, a call option buyer is purchasing a contract that gives them the right to buy shares of stock at the value of the strike price. Since the 45 strike call option is below the current stock price, the option seller must collect at least the intrinsic value of the option in order for the trade to be practical.

Why would the option seller agree to give up shares of stock for less than the current market value? If the option seller could only receive $3 to give another investor the right to buy their shares of stock for $4 less then the market price, no one would trade options. This is why the option premium must at least equal the intrinsic value of the option strike price.

The same philosophies apply to the put option. In Figure 1.3, the 55 strike put option has an ask price of $5.50. Since XYZ is trading at $50, the 55 strike put option is 5 points ITM, or has $5 of intrinsic value. A put option buyer is purchasing the right to sell shares of stock at the value of the strike price. The put option seller, who is obligated to buy the shares of stock, must collect at least the intrinsic value for the trade to be fair. Why would the put option seller agree to buy shares of stock for a higher price than the current market value if they did not receive adequate compensation?

Out-of-the-money (OTM) options do not have intrinsic value. The premium for OTM options is comprised completely of time value.

Time value refers to the dollar amount the option buyer is paying for the time until the expiration date, and the option seller is collecting for the time to expiration.

In the example we used:

- Stock XYZ is trading at $50.

- The 45 call has an ask price of $5.40.

- The 45 call is 5 points ITM. ($50 – $45).

- The remaining $0.40 is the *time value* for that option.

The $0.40 represents the premium the call option buyer pays for the right to buy shares of stock any time during the next 30 days. This means that the call option buyer is paying slightly more than $0.01 per day for the right to buy the shares of XYZ at $45 per share ($0.40 time value / 30 days remaining to expiration = $0.0133 per day).

For the 55 strike put option:

- Stock XYZ is trading at $50.

- The 55 put option has an ask price of $5.50.

- The 55 put option is 5 points ITM ($55 - $50).

- The remaining $0.50 is the time value for that option.

The $0.50 represents the premium the put option buyer will pay for the right to sell shares of stock during the next 30 days. Basically, the put option buyer is paying almost $0.02 per day for this right ($0.50 time value / 30 days remaining to expiration = $0.0166 per day).

For OTM options, the listed price is the time value for that option. In Figure 1.3, the ask price for the 55 strike call option is $0.30. Remember, the 55 call option is OTM because the stock is currently trading below the strike price. The 55 call option has no intrinsic value. An investor who purchases the 55 call option is speculating on a sudden rise in the stock to make a profit. If XYZ were still trading at $50 at expiration, the 55 call option would expire worthless. The call buyer would not exercise the right to purchase shares of stock at $55 when shares could be purchased directly on the market for less. If the

PUTTING CONCEPTS TOGETHER

Earlier in this chapter, the option series for optionable stocks were discussed. The concepts of time value were just discussed.

Question: If an investor buys or sells an option with a further out expiration date, do they have to pay or collect more for that option?

Answer: Yes. Options that are bought or sold further out in time will have a higher time value for the same strike price.

call option expires worthless, the long call option speculator would lose the full amount of the call option purchase price.

In Figure 1.3, the ask price for the OTM 45 put option is $0.40. The put option is OTM because the stock price is trading above the put option strike price. An investor who purchased the 45 put is speculating that the stock will drop in price. If XYZ falls below $45, the put option buyer can force the put seller to buy shares of stock for a higher value than the market price. If XYZ remains at $50 or rises, the 45 put option will expire worthless. The put option buyer would not exercise the right to sell shares of stock at $45 when the shares could be sold at the market price for a higher value.

As expiration day approaches, the time value on all options will decay. At expiration, any ITM options, whether they are call options or put options, will only retain their intrinsic value, and all

Figure 1.4: Option Chain Stock XYZ Trading at $50

More Info	Strike	Opt Bid	Opt Ask	Time Value	% Time Value	Opt Bid	Opt Ask	Time Value	% Time Value
Stock (XYZ) $50.00				Near Month Options - 30 days to expiration					
▶	40.00	9.70	10.50	-0.08	-0.2%	0.00	0.15	-	-
▶	45.00	5.10	5.50	0.32	0.6%	0.25	0.40	0.25	0.5%
▶	50.00	1.55	1.80	1.55	3.1%	1.60	1.85	1.38	2.8%
▶	55.00	0.15	0.30	0.15	0.3%	5.10	5.50	-0.12	-0.2%
▶	60.00	0.00	0.10	-	-	9.80	10.40	-0.42	-0.8%
Stock (XYZ) $50.00				4 Month Out Options - 120 days to expiration					
▶	35.00	15.10	15.60	0.32	0.6%	0.10	0.25	0.10	0.2%
▶	40.00	10.40	11.10	0.62	1.2%	0.40	0.55	0.40	0.8%
▶	45.00	6.40	6.70	1.62	3.3%	1.20	1.40	1.20	2.4%
▶	50.00	3.10	3.50	3.10	6.2%	2.90	3.20	2.68	5.4%
▶	55.00	1.20	1.40	1.20	2.4%	5.90	6.30	0.68	1.4%
▶	60.00	0.30	0.50	0.30	0.6%	10.10	10.50	-0.12	-0.2%

Source: PowerOptions (www.poweropt.com)

OTM options will expire worthless, as they no longer have any inherent value.

Figure 1.4 shows the XYZ chain again, this time with the time value and *percent time value* (the time value amount represented as a percentage of the underlying stock price) amounts shown for different expiration months.

Figure 1.4 shows the time value for the near month 50 call option (30 days left to expiration) is $1.55.

The corresponding four month out 50 call option (120 days left to expiration) has a time value of $3.10.

A call seller would collect an additional $1.55 of time value for 90 more days until the option reaches expiration. Time value is the fee collected by the writer and the added cost that is paid by the option buyer. Time value works for the option seller as the premium decays over time, and conversely, time value works against an option buyer.

PUTTING CONCEPTS TOGETHER

Notice in Figure 1.4 that the at-the-money options, those closest to the stock price, have the highest time value in each month. The near month 50 strike call option and the 50 strike put option have a time value of 3.1% and 2.8% respectively, and the four month out 50 strike call and 50 strike put have time values of 6.2% and 5.4%. The ATM options will always have the highest time value for an optionable stock.

IMPORTANT CONCEPTS FROM THE INTRODUCTION SECTION

Table 1.1 showed the rights and obligations of an option buyer and option seller, and Table 1.2 showed the market sentiment of each action. But these were for uncovered positions where the investor does not own or has not shorted shares of stock.

Remember, when an investor buys a put option, they have purchased the right to sell the shares of stock at the strike price. The put option acts as insurance for the underlying security. The stock could drop to $0.00 in value, but the put owner can still sell the shares of stock for the value of the put strike price.

When an investor sells a call option, they are obligated to deliver shares of stock at the strike price. If an investor sells a call option without owning a stock, it is called a naked call. The naked call strategy is a neutral to bearish strategy. When an investor sells a call against shares that they own, it is called a covered call trade. Since the stock is owned, the investor benefits when the stock moves up. The covered call trade is a neutral to bullish strategy, as the investor now wants the stock to go up in price; however, in the covered call strategy, the investor is only protected by the amount of premium they receive when they sell the call. This may only be about 2 or 3 percent of the underlying share price. When an investor sells the call option and purchases a put option, the premium received from the sale of the call option will pay for or reduce the price of the put option. The investor has limited the maximum risk on the position by purchasing the put option and has generated income by selling the call option.

REVIEW QUESTIONS FOR CHAPTER 1

1. The iron condor stock options strategy performs best in which kind of market?

   A. Bearish

   B. Bullish

   C. Neutral

   D. None of the above

2. Iron condor traders should:

   A. Invest all of their capital with iron condors

   B. Trade when market volatility is low

   C. Trade when market volatility is high following a market-moving event

   D. None of the above

3. The best time to enter an iron condor trade was just before:

   A. 9/11

   B. Hurricane Katrina

   C. Lehman Brother bankruptcy

   D. None of the above

4. Purchasing a call option is considered what type of position?

   A. Bearish

   B. Bullish

   C. Neutral

   D. None of the above

5. Purchasing a put option is considered what type of position?

   A. Bearish

   B. Bullish

   C. Neutral

   D. None of the above

6. Sellers of stock options:

   A. Have no obligations

   B. Have obligations

   C. Are considered stock brokers

   D. None of the above

7. The strike price for a call option represents

   A. The price at which the buyer of a call option has the right to purchase the security

   B. The price at which the buyer of a call option has the right to sell the security

   C. The price when the bell rings

   D. None of the above

8. A call option's strike price that is lower than the underlying price of the security is considered:

   A. In-the-money (ITM)

   B. Out-of-the-money (OTM)

   C. At-the-money (ATM)

   D. None of the above

9. A call option's strike price that is higher than the underlying price of the security is considered:

    A. In-the-money (ITM)

    B. Out-of-the-money (OTM)

    C. At-the-money (ATM)

    D. None of the above

10. A security price very close to the price of a call option's strike is considered:

    A. In-the-money (ITM)

    B. Out-of-the-money (OTM)

    C. At-the-money (ATM)

    D. None of the above

11. One option contract typically represents:

    A. 10 shares of the underlying equity

    B. 100 shares of the underlying equity

    C. 1,000 shares of the underlying equity

    D. None of the above

 Go to the Traders' Library Education Corner at www.traderslibrary.com/TLEcorner for answers to these self-test questions.

Chapter 2

THEORY BEHIND
THE IRON CONDOR

An iron condor position is a neutral options strategy that best performs when markets or the underlying equities remain stagnant or trade within a specific range. The profit and loss diagram for an iron condor at option expiration is shown in Figure 2.1.

Entry of an iron condor position consists of selling two short options and purchasing two long options. If the price of the underlying equity at expiration is between the strike prices of the short options, the iron condor will be fully profitable, as illustrated in Figure 2.2.

A break-even point represents the price of an underlying equity at which a position will neither generate a profit nor experience a loss. If the price of the underlying at expiration is between the break-even point and the short option strike price, the iron condor will return a profit, but not the maximum potential profit. Partial profit for an iron condor is illustrated in Figure 2.3.

At options expiration, an underlying price which is between the break-even point and the long option strike price, will be cause a loss, but not a complete loss, as illustrated by Figure 2.4.

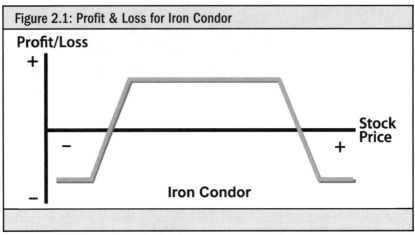

Figure 2.1: Profit & Loss for Iron Condor

Profit/Loss

+

Stock
Price

−

+

Iron Condor

−

Source: PowerOptions (www.poweropt.com)

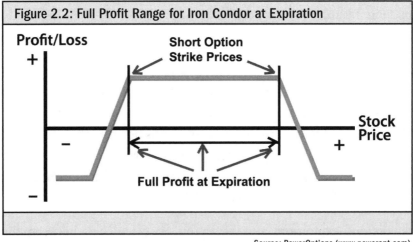

Figure 2.2: Full Profit Range for Iron Condor at Expiration

Profit/Loss

+

Short Option
Strike Prices

Stock
Price

−

+

Full Profit at Expiration

−

Source: PowerOptions (www.poweropt.com)

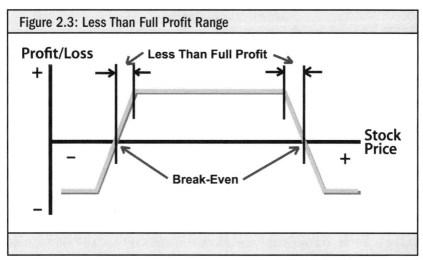

Figure 2.3: Less Than Full Profit Range

Source: PowerOptions (www.poweropt.com)

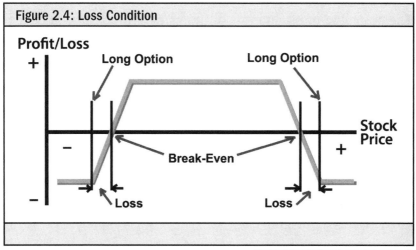

Figure 2.4: Loss Condition

Source: PowerOptions (www.poweropt.com)

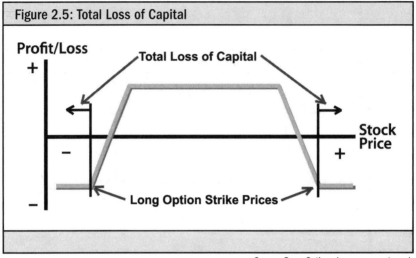

Figure 2.5: Total Loss of Capital

Profit/Loss

Total Loss of Capital

Stock Price

Long Option Strike Prices

Source: PowerOptions (www.poweropt.com)

If the price of the underlying at expiration is less than the strike price of the long put option or greater than the strike price of the long call option, the iron condor will sustain a total loss of invested capital as illustrated in Figure 2.5.

The preceding profit and loss diagrams have been for iron condor positions at expiration. The profit and loss for an iron condor is dynamic and varies depending upon a number of variables. A large portion of the variability of the profit and loss for an iron condor is dependant upon the length of time following initial entry. A profit and loss comparison diagram for an iron condor immediately following initial entry is shown in Figure 2.6.

Due to the large bid-ask spread of an iron condor, exit of an iron condor immediately following initial entry will guarantee sustaining a loss as shown in Figure 2.6.

A profit and loss comparison diagram for an iron condor near the halfway point to expiration is shown in Figure 2.7.

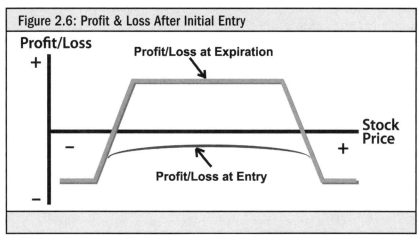

Figure 2.6: Profit & Loss After Initial Entry

Source: PowerOptions (www.poweropt.com)

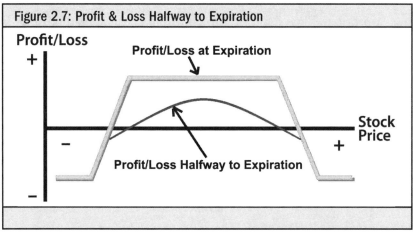

Figure 2.7: Profit & Loss Halfway to Expiration

Source: PowerOptions (www.poweropt.com)

As illustrated in Figure 2.7, the iron condor generally becomes more profitable as the time to expiration decreases. This phenomenon is a result of the decay in time value for the short options. The longer an iron condor position has been held, the smaller the penalty experienced from an early exit.

CREDIT SPREADS

An iron condor position is constructed by combining two popular leveraged options strategies: the *bull-put credit spread* and the *bear-call credit spread*. A credit spread trade is entered through the sale of an option in conjunction with the purchase of another option. The sum of the sale and purchase is a credit, hence the moniker *credit* spread.

Bull-Put Credit Spread

A bull-put credit spread performs best when the market is neutral-to-bullish or the price of the underlying equity is stagnant to increasing. A profit and loss diagram for a bull-put credit spread position is shown in Figure 2.8.

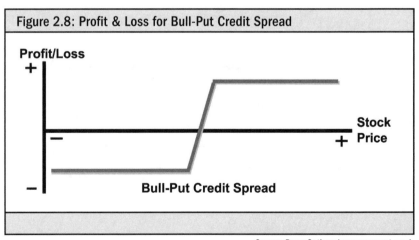

Figure 2.8: Profit & Loss for Bull-Put Credit Spread

Source: PowerOptions (www.poweropt.com)

A bull-put credit spread consists of selling a put option at- or out-of-the-money, while at the same time purchasing a deeper out-of-the-money put option with the same expiration date.

An example of a put option chain for the OEX index is shown in Figure 2.9.

To enter a bull-put credit spread for OEX, we could sell to open put option OEWQI (MAY 345) for $2.25 per share of the underlying security and buy to open put option OEWQG (MAY 335) for $1.85 per share of the underlying security. Both put options expire in May.

Put option OEWQI (MAY 345) has a strike price of $345 and put option OEWQG (MAY 335) has a strike price of $335. The short put option technically obligates an investor to receive shares of the underlying at $345, and the long put option provides an investor the right to sell shares of the underlying at $335.

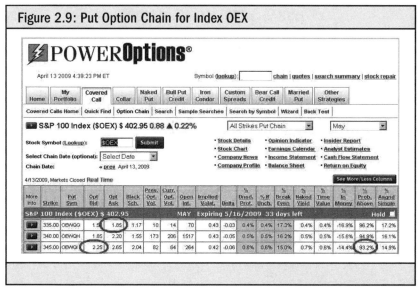

Figure 2.9: Put Option Chain for Index OEX

Source: PowerOptions (www.poweropt.com)

In this case, the underlying is an index and the options are cash settled instead of actual shares being transferred as a result of option exercise. For this position, an investor is at risk for the 10-point spread between the short and long put options. If the price of OEX were less than $335 at expiration, an investor would realize a loss of the 10-point spread minus the initial credit. The net credit per share of the security for entering the bull-put credit spread would be $1.85 subtracted from $2.25, or $0.40. The initial margin requirement would be the net credit subtracted from the difference between the strike prices of the options, sold and purchased, multiplied by a quantity of 100 and multiplied times the number of contracts.

Margin Requirement for Bull-Put Credit Spread

= [(Short Put Option Strike – Long Put Option Strike) – Bull-Put Net Credit] * # of contracts * 100 shares/contract

For this particular bull-put credit spread example, the initial margin requirement for one contract would be $960 and is calculated as:

$$[(\$345 - \$335) - \$0.40] * 1 * 100 =$$
$$[(\$10) - \$0.40] * 100 =$$
$$[\$9.60] * 100 =$$
$$\$960$$

As indicated in Figure 2.9, the theoretical probability that the price of OEX will be greater than the strike price of OEWQI (MAY 345) at options expiration is 93.2 percent. This means the position has a theoretical 93.2 percent chance that both the options expire worthless, achieving full profit with the investor not having to fulfill any obligations related to the option contracts.

Here is the calculation for the maximum potential return for the bull-put credit spread.

Bull-Put Credit Maximum Potential Return =

$$\frac{\text{initial net credit/share * 100 shares/contract * \# contracts}}{\text{margin requirement}}$$

The maximum potential return for the bull-put credit spread per one contract position would be:

Bull-Put Credit Spread Maximum Potential Return =

$$\frac{\$0.40 * 100 * 1}{\$960} = 4.17\%$$

A return of this magnitude can generally be experienced in one month or less for a bull-put credit spread. However, there is also the potential for experiencing a loss.

The maximum potential loss for the bull-put is 100 percent of the margin requirement. A bull-put position experiencing the maximum loss would retain the initial credit, but would incur a loss of the entire amount of the margin requirement.

The 4.17 percent return would be fully realized at options expiration in May provided the closing price of the index OEX is greater than the sold put option's strike price of $345. For prices of OEX greater than $345, both put options, sold and purchased, are out-of-the-money and will expire worthless with the investment returning a profit of the initial net credit of $0.40 per share of the underlying security, or $40 per contract.

For prices of OEX less than $345, the bull-put credit spread position does not experience the maximum potential return. For prices of OEX less than the break-even of $344.60 (the sold strike price minus the initial net credit ($345-$0.40)), the position experiences a loss. If the price of OEX closes less than the purchased put option strike price of $335, the position experiences a total loss of margin requirement of $960 per contract. Table 2.1 illustrates the three corner case conditions for profit and loss for the example bull-put position.

Table 2.1: Profit and Loss Corner Cases for Bull-Put Credit Spread

Date		Price OEX	Long Put Price OEWQG MAY 335	Short Put Price OEWQI MAY 345	Total Profit/Loss per Contract	Percent Return
4/13/2009		$402.95	$1.85	$2.25		
5/16/2009*		>=$345	$0	$0		
	Profit/Loss		$(1.85)	$2.25	$0.40	4.17%
5/16/2009*		$344.60	$0	$0.40		
	Profit/Loss		$(1.85)	$1.85	$0.00	0%
5/16/2009*		$335	$0	$10		
	Profit/Loss		$(1.85)	($7.75)	$(9.60)	(100%)
* options expiration						

A profit and loss diagram for this particular bull-put position is shown in Figure 2.10.

The maximum potential profit of 4.17 percent is realized if OEX is greater than or equal to $345 at options expiration on May 16, 2009. For OEX greater than $345 at expiration, both short and long options expire worthless. The short put option produces a profit of $2.25 calculated as the expiration price of $0 subtracted from the initial sold price of $2.25. The long put option produces a loss of -$1.85 calculated as the initial purchase price of $1.85 subtracted from the

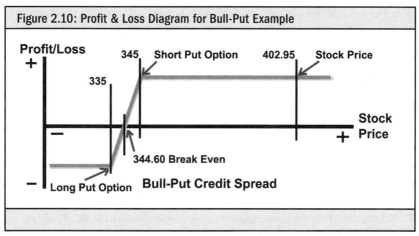

Figure 2.10: Profit & Loss Diagram for Bull-Put Example

Profit/Loss
345 Short Put Option   402.95 Stock Price

335

Stock + Price

344.60 Break Even

Long Put Option **Bull-Put Credit Spread**

Source: PowerOptions (www.poweropt.com)

expiration price of $0. The net profit of $0.40 is calculated as the difference between the profit sustained for the short put option and the loss sustained for the long put option, or $2.25-$1.85. The total loss of -$9.60 is calculated as the combined loss from the long put option and the short put option, or -$1.85-$7.75.

The trade breaks even at an expiration price of $344.60. For an expiration price of OEX at $344.60, the long put option expires worthless, generating a loss of -$1.85. The short put option has an expiration value of $0.40, resulting in a profit of $1.85. The profit of $1.85 is calculated as the expiration price of $0.40 subtracted from the initial sold price of $2.25. The difference between the profit generated for the short put option and the loss sustained for the long put ($1.85 - $1.85) results in a net profit/loss of $0.

For expiration prices of OEX less than $344.60 and greater than $335, a partial loss of capital is experienced. The closer the expiration price is to $335, the larger the loss.

A total loss of $9.60 per underlying equity of the contract is sustained for prices of OEX less than or equal to $335 at expiration. At an expiration price of $335, the long put option expires worthless and sustains a loss of -$1.85 calculated as the initial purchase price of $1.85 subtracted from the expiration price of $0. The short put option realizes a loss of -$7.75 calculated as the spread between the short and long options of $10 ($345-$335) subtracted from the initial sold price of the short put option of $2.25, or $2.25 - $10.

The OEX index would have to drop approximately 15 percent in price at expiration before this position becomes a loss and drop about 17 percent before the position becomes a total loss. The OEX index is a broad based market index and the chance of a drop of greater than 15 percent to 17 percent over about 30 days is highly unlikely. Once the OEX drops 15 percent, however, the resulting loss from further movement can occur very rapidly with continued downward movement of the OEX index.

Bear-Call Credit Spread

A bear-call credit spread performs best when the market is neutral-to-bearish or the price of the underlying equity is stagnant or decreases. A profit and loss diagram for a bear-call credit spread position is shown in Figure 2.11.

A bear-call credit spread is created by selling an at-the-money or out-of-the-money call option, while at the same time purchasing a deeper out-of-the-money call option with the same expiration date. An example call option chain for the OEX index is shown in Figure 2.12.

To enter a bear-call credit spread for OEX, OXBEJ (MAY 450) call option would be sold to open for $1.80 per share of the underly-

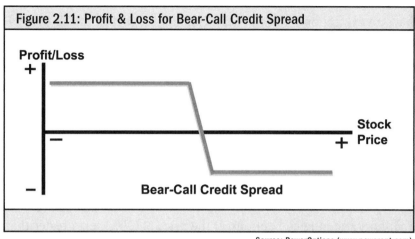

Figure 2.11: Profit & Loss for Bear-Call Credit Spread

Source: PowerOptions (www.poweropt.com)

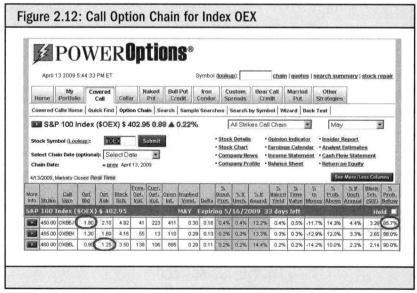

Figure 2.12: Call Option Chain for Index OEX

Source: PowerOptions (www.poweropt.com)

ing security, and OXBEL (MAY 460) call option would be bought to open for $1.25 per share of the underlying security. Both options have an expiration month of May. Call option OXBEJ (MAY 450) has a strike price of $450 and call option OXBEL (MAY 460) has a strike price of $460. The short call option technically obligates an investor to deliver shares of the underlying at $450, and the long call option provides an investor the right to purchase shares of the underlying at $460. In this case, the underlying is an index and the options are cash settled instead of actual shares being transferred as a result of option exercise.

For this position, an investor is at risk for the 10-point spread between the short and long call options. If the price of OEX were greater than $460 at expiration, an investor would realize a loss for the 10-point spread minus the initial credit. The net credit per share of the security for entering the bear-call credit spread would be $1.25 subtracted from $1.80, or $0.55. The initial margin requirement would be the net credit subtracted from the difference between the strike prices of the options, sold and purchased, multiplied by a quantity of 100 and multiplied times the number of contracts.

Margin Requirement for Bull-Put Credit Spread

= [(Long Call Option Strike – Short Call Option Strike) – Bear-Call Net Credit] * # of contracts * 100 shares/contract

For the bear-call credit spread example, the initial margin requirement would be $945, calculated as:

$$[(\$460-\$450)-\$0.55]*1*100 =$$
$$[(\$10)-\$0.55]*100 =$$
$$[\$9.45]*100 =$$
$$\$945$$

The theoretical probability that the price of OEX will be less than $450, the short call option strike price for OXBEJ (MAY 450), at options expiration is provided in Figure 2.12 as the Percent Probability Below, which is shown to be 85.7 percent. This means the position has a theoretical 85.7 percent chance that both the call options will expire worthless and achieve full profitability with the investor not having to fulfill any obligations related to the option contracts.

The calculation for the maximum potential return for the bear-call credit spread is the same as for the bull-put credit spread. The maximum potential return of the bear-call credit spread for this example for a one contract position would be calculated as:

Bear-Call Credit Spread Maximum Potential Return =

$$\frac{\$0.55*100*1}{\$945} = 5.82\%$$

The 5.82 percent return would be fully realized at options expiration in May, provided the OEX index closes below the sold call option's strike price of $450. For prices of OEX less than or equal to $450, both call options, sold and purchased, are out-of-the-money and will expire worthless. The investor will keep the initial net credit of $0.55 per share of the underlying security as profit.

For prices of OEX greater than $450, the bear-call credit spread position does not experience the maximum potential return. For prices of OEX greater than the break-even of $450.55 (the sold strike price plus the initial net credit ($450+$0.55)), the position experiences a loss. If the price of OEX closes greater than the purchased call option strike price of $460, the position experiences a total loss of capital, or $945 per contract. Table 2.2 illustrates the profit/loss corner cases for the bear-call credit spread position.

Table 2.2: Profit and Loss Corner Cases for Bear-Call Credit Spread

Date		Price OEX	Short Call Price OXBEJ MAY 450	Long Call Price OEWQG MAY 460	Total Profit/ Loss per Contract	Percent Return
4/13/2009		$402.95	$1.80	$1.25		
5/16/2009		<=$450	$0	$0		
	Profit/Loss		$1.80	$(1.25)	$0.55	5.82%
5/16/2009		$450.55	$0.55	$0		
	Profit/Loss		$1.25	$(1.25)	$0	0%
5/16/2009		$460	$10	$0		
	Profit/Loss		$(8.20)	$(1.25)	$(9.45)	(100%)

A profit and loss diagram for the example bear-call credit spread is shown in Figure 2.13.

The maximum potential profit of 5.82 percent is realized if OEX is less than or equal to $450 at expiration. With OEX less than or equal to $450 at expiration, the short call option expires worthless, resulting in a profit for the option of $1.80, which is calculated as the expiration price of $0 subtracted from the initial sold price of $1.80.

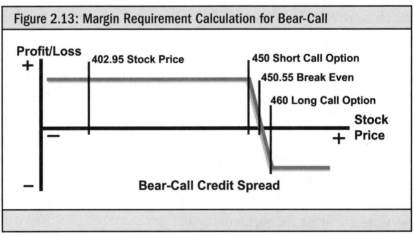

Figure 2.13: Margin Requirement Calculation for Bear-Call

Profit/Loss
402.95 Stock Price
450 Short Call Option
450.55 Break Even
460 Long Call Option
Stock Price
Bear-Call Credit Spread

Source: PowerOptions (www.poweropt.com)

The long option expires worthless, resulting in a loss for the option of -$1.25, which is calculated as the expiration price of $0 subtracted from the initial purchase price of $1.25. A net profit of $0.55 is experienced for the bear-call, which is calculated as the difference between the profit of $1.80 for the short call option and the loss of -$1.25 for the long call option.

The trade breaks even at an expiration price for OEX of $450.55. The price of the short call option at expiration is $0.55 and the long call option expires worthless. A $1.25 profit is experienced for the short call option, calculated as the expiration price of $0.55 subtracted from the initial sold price of $1.80. A loss of -$1.25 is sustained for the long call option, calculated as the expiration price of $0 subtracted from the initial purchase price of $1.25. The resulting net profit of $0 is calculated as the difference between the profit for the short call option of $1.25 and the loss for the long call option of -$1.25.

The position sustains a partial loss for prices of OEX of greater than $450.55 and less than $460 at expiration. The closer the price of OEX to $460 at expiration, the larger the loss sustained.

The position sustains a total loss of $9.45 per underlying equity of the contract for prices of OEX greater than $460. A price of $460 for OEX at expiration results in a price for the short call option of $10 with the long call option expiring worthless. The short call option sustains a loss of -$8.20, calculated as the short call's expiration price of $10 subtracted from the long call's initial sold price of $1.80. The long call option sustains a loss of -$1.25, calculated as the call option's initial purchase price of $1.25 subtracted from the call option's expiration price of $0. The resulting loss of -$9.45 is the combined loss for the short call option of -$8.20 and the loss for the long call option of -$1.25.

BULL-PUT CREDIT SPREAD + BEAR-CALL CREDIT SPREAD = IRON CONDOR

The iron condor position is simply the combination of a bull-put credit spread and a bear-call credit spread, as illustrated in Figure 2.14.

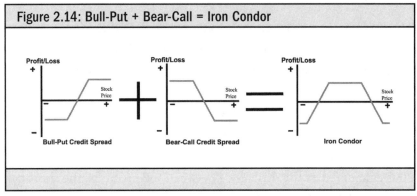

Figure 2.14: Bull-Put + Bear-Call = Iron Condor

Source: PowerOptions (www.poweropt.com)

Combining the previous bull-put and bear-call positions to create an iron condor is illustrated in Table 2.3.

Table 2.3: Bull-Put + Bear-Call = Iron Condor

Transaction/Net Credit	Equity	Price	
Buy to Open	OEWQG May 335 Put	$1.85	
Sell to Open	OEWQI May 345 Put	$2.25	
Net Credit Bull-Put		$0.40	$0.40
Sell to Open	OXBEJ MAY 450 Call	$1.80	
Buy to Open	OEWQG May 460 Call	$1.25	
Net Credit Bear-Call		$0.55	$0.55
Net Credit Iron Condor			$0.95

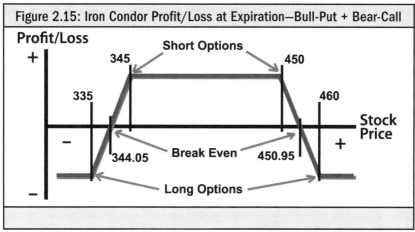

Figure 2.15: Iron Condor Profit/Loss at Expiration—Bull-Put + Bear-Call

The $0.40 net credit received for the bull-put combined with the $0.55 net credit received for the bear-call results in a total net credit for the iron condor of $0.95.

A profit and loss diagram resulting from combining the previous bull-put and bear-call to create an iron condor is shown in Figure 2.15.

The initial margin requirement would be the net credits subtracted from the differences between the strike prices of the put and call options, sold and purchased, multiplied by a quantity of 100 and multiplied times the number of contracts.

Margin Requirement for Iron Condor

= [{(Short Put Option Strike – Long Put Option Strike) + (Long Call Option Strike – Short Call Option Strike)} – (Bull-Put Net Credit + Bear-Call Net Credit)]* # contracts * 100 shares/contract

The margin requirement for one contract of the iron condor example is $1,905 and would be calculated as:

$$[\{(\$345\text{-}\$335) + (\$460\text{-}\$450)\} - (\$0.40\text{+}\$0.55)] * 1 * 100 =$$
$$[\$10 + \$10 - \$0.95] * 100 =$$
$$\$1,905$$

Based on a combined margin requirement for the example bull-put and bear-call positions, the return for the iron condor as a result of combining the bull-put credit spread and the bear-call credit spread for a one contract position would be calculated as:

Iron Condor Maximum Potential Return=

$$\frac{(\$0.40\text{+}\$0.55) * 100 * 1}{\$1,905} = 4.99\%$$

For a special subset of iron condors with selected brokers, the margin requirement is *not* the combined margins of the bull-put credit spread and the bear-call credit spread, but rather the margin requirement is considered for only the bull-put credit spread *or* the bear-call credit spread. The reason behind the allowance for a special margin requirement is the iron condor can only suffer a loss for either the bull-put credit spread or the bear-call credit spread, but not both. Not all brokers support special margin for iron condor trades. Traders desiring to trade iron condors with special margin should verify that their broker supports special margin before entering trades. In general, an iron condor position with options having identical expiration months and with an identical margin requirement for the bull-put credit spread position and the bear-call credit spread position will be considered as special, with brokers allowing special margin for the positions.

The special margin calculation for the example iron condor would be $905 calculated as:

$$[\$10 - \$0.95] * 1 * 100 = \$905.$$

An alternate calculation for the maximum potential return of the iron condor with special margin considerations is:

Iron Condor Maximum Potential Return =

$$\frac{\text{initial net credit per contract * 100 shares/contract * \# contacts}}{\text{margin requirement}}$$

For the previous example, the calculation for the iron condor return using special margin requirement for one contact would be calculated.

Iron Condor Maximum Potential Return=

$$\frac{(\$0.40+\$0.55) * 100 * 1}{\$1,905} = 4.99\%$$

As illustrated in Table 2.4, the maximum potential return for the special margin case of the iron condor exhibited a return of a little more than double the return of the calculation based on general margin consideration.

Table 2.4: Comparison of Iron Condor with and without Special Margin

Return without Special Margin	Return with Special Margin
4.9%	10.5%

Table 2.5: Maximum Potential Return for Iron Condors Based on Strike Difference and Net Credit

Net Credit per Contract	Separation Among Option Strike Prices														
	$1	$2	$3	$4	$5	$6	$7	$8	$9	$10	$15	$20	$25	$50	$100
$0.05	5.3%	2.6%	1.7%	1.3%	1%	0.8%	0.7%	0.6%	0.6%	0.5%	0.3%	0.3%	0.2%	0.1%	0.1%
$0.10	11.1%	5.3%	3.4%	2.6%	2%	1.7%	1.4%	1.3%	1.1%	1%	0.7%	0.5%	0.4%	0.2%	0.1%
$0.15	17.6%	8.1%	5.3%	3.9%	3.1%	2.6%	2.2%	1.9%	1.7%	1.5%	1.0%	0.8%	0.6%	0.3%	0.2%
$0.20	25.0%	11.1%	7.1%	5.3%	4.2%	3.4%	2.9%	2.6%	2.3%	2%	1.4%	1.0%	0.8%	0.4%	0.2%
$0.25	33.3%	14.3%	9.1%	6.7%	5.3%	4.3%	3.7%	3.2%	2.9%	2.6%	1.7%	1.3%	1.0%	0.5%	0.3%
$0.30	42.9%	17.6%	11.1%	8.1%	6.4%	5.3%	4.5%	3.9%	3.4%	3.1%	2%	1.5%	1.2%	0.6%	0.3%
$0.35	53.8%	21.2%	13.2%	9.6%	7.5%	6.2%	5.3%	4.6%	4.0%	3.6%	2.4%	1.8%	1.4%	0.7%	0.4%
$0.40	66.7%	25%	15.4%	11.1%	8.7%	7.1%	6.1%	5.3%	4.7%	4.2%	2.7%	2%	1.6%	0.8%	0.4%
$0.45	81.8%	29%	17.6%	12.7%	9.9%	8.1%	6.9%	6%	5.3%	4.7%	3.1%	2.3%	1.8%	0.9%	0.5%
$0.50	100%	33.3%	20%	14.3%	11.1%	9.1%	7.7%	6.7%	5.9%	5.3%	3.4%	2.6%	2%	1%	0.5%
$0.55		37.9%	22.4%	15.9%	12.4%	10.1%	8.5%	7.4%	6.5%	5.8%	3.8%	2.8%	2.2%	1.1%	0.6%
$0.60		42.9%	25%	17.6%	13.6%	11.1%	9.4%	8.1%	7.1%	6.4%	4.2%	3.1%	2.5%	1.2%	0.6%
$0.65		48.1%	27.7%	19.4%	14.9%	12.1%	10.2%	8.8%	7.8%	7.0%	4.5%	3.4%	2.7%	1.3%	0.7%
$0.70		53.8%	30.4%	21.2%	16.3%	13.2%	11.1%	9.6%	8.4%	7.5%	4.9%	3.6%	2.9%	1.4%	0.7%
$0.75		60%	33.3%	23.1%	17.6%	14.3%	12.0%	10.3%	9.1%	8.1%	5.3%	3.9%	3.1%	1.5%	0.8%
$0.80		66.7%	36.4%	25%	19%	15.4%	12.9%	11.1%	9.8%	8.7%	5.6%	4.2%	3.3%	1.6%	0.8%
$0.85		73.9%	39.5%	27.0%	20.5%	16.5%	13.8%	11.9%	10.4%	9.3%	6.0%	4.4%	3.5%	1.7%	0.9%
$0.90		81.8%	42.9%	29.0%	22%	17.6%	14.8%	12.7%	11.1%	9.9%	6.4%	4.7%	3.7%	1.8%	0.9%

$0.95	1%	1.9%	4%	5%	6.8%	10.5%	11.8%	13.5%	15.7%	18.8%	23.5%	31.1%	46.3%	90.5%
$1.00	1.0%	2%	4.2%	5.3%	7.1%	11.1%	12.5%	14.3%	16.7%	20%	25.0%	33.3%	50%	100%
$1.05	1.1%	2.1%	4.4%	5.5%	7.5%	11.7%	13.2%	15.1%	17.6%	21.2%	26.6%	35.6%	53.8%	
$1.10	1.1%	2.2%	4.6%	5.8%	7.9%	12.4%	13.9%	15.9%	18.6%	22.4%	28.2%	37.9%	57.9%	
$1.15	1.2%	2.4%	4.8%	6.1%	8.3%	13%	14.6%	16.8%	19.7%	23.7%	29.9%	40.4%	62.2%	
$1.20	1.2%	2.5%	5%	6.4%	8.7%	13.6%	15.4%	17.6%	20.7%	25%	31.6%	42.9%	66.7%	
$1.25	1.3%	2.6%	5.3%	6.7%	9.1%	14.3%	16.1%	18.5%	21.7%	26.3%	33.3%	45.5%	71.4%	
$1.30	1.3%	2.7%	5.5%	7%	9.5%	14.9%	16.9%	19.4%	22.8%	27.7%	35.1%	48.1%	76.5%	
$1.35	1.4%	2.8%	5.7%	7.2%	9.9%	15.6%	17.6%	20.3%	23.9%	29%	37%	50.9%	81.8%	
$1.40	1.4%	2.9%	5.9%	7.5%	10.3%	16.3%	18.4%	21.2%	25.0%	30.4%	38.9%	53.8%	87.5%	
$1.45	1.5%	3%	6.2%	7.8%	10.7%	17%	19.2%	22.1%	26.1%	31.9%	40.8%	56.9%	93.5%	
$1.50	1.5%	3.1%	6.4%	8.1%	11.1%	17.6%	20%	23.1%	27.3%	33.3%	42.9%	60.0%	100%	
$1.55	1.6%	3.2%	6.6%	8.4%	11.5%	18.3%	20.8%	24%	28.4%	34.8%	44.9%	63.3%		
$1.60	1.6%	3.3%	6.8%	8.7%	11.9%	19%	21.6%	25%	29.6%	36.4%	47.1%	66.7%		
$1.65	1.7%	3.4%	7.1%	9%	12.4%	19.8%	22.4%	26%	30.8%	37.9%	49.3%	70.2%		
$1.70	1.7%	3.5%	7.3%	9.3%	12.8%	20.5%	23.3%	27%	32.1%	39.5%	51.5%	73.9%		
$1.75	1.8%	3.6%	7.5%	9.6%	13.2%	21.2%	24.1%	28%	33.3%	41.2%	53.8%	77.8%		
$1.80	1.8%	3.7%	7.8%	9.9%	13.6%	22.0%	25.0%	29%	34.6%	42.9%	56.3%	81.8%		
$1.85	1.9%	3.8%	8%	10.2%	14.1%	22.7%	25.9%	30.1%	35.9%	44.6%	58.7%	86%		
$1.90	1.9%	4.0%	8.2%	10.5%	14.5%	23.5%	26.8%	31.1%	37.3%	46.3%	61.3%	90.5%		
$1.95	2%	4.1%	8.5%	10.8%	14.9%	24.2%	27.7%	32.2%	38.6%	48.1%	63.9%	95.1%		
$2.00	2%	4.2%	8.7%	11.1%	15.4%	25%	28.6%	33.3%	40%	50%	66.7%	100%		

Table 2.5 has been provided for ease of determining the return of an iron condor with special margin considerations based on the difference between the option strike prices and the net credit per contract.

Table 2.5 can also be used for calculating the Maximum Potential Returns for bull-put and bear-call credit spreads.

PARTIAL SUCCESS

Iron condors can always be considered at least partially successful, as either the bull-put or the bear-call will always be profitable. The underlying security can only violate the short strike of either the bull-put or the bear-call, but not both simultaneously. In cases where a partial loss was sustained for one of the option spreads as a result of experiencing a stop-loss (see Chapter 5), the profitable option spread may generate enough income to maintain an overall profit for the iron condor. Table 2.6 illustrates the corner case profit and loss for the iron condor example.

STATISTICS AND PROBABILITY OF IRON CONDORS

In general, statistical financial calculations for stock options are based on the assumption that the behavior of the stock market is *Gaussian* or *Normal*, as illustrated by the familiar curve shown in Figure 2.16.

A Gaussian probability distribution for the stock market would infer that the stock market experiences random price movements varying about the mean. As can be seen in Figure 2.16, a stock market exhibiting Gaussian behavior would rarely experience large price movements. Unfortunately, the actual behavior or distribution of the stock market is not Gaussian. The actual behavior of the stock market performs closer to the distribution as shown in Figure 2.17.

Table 2.6: Profit and Loss Corner Cases for Iron Condor

Date		Price OEX	Price OEWQG MAY 335	Price OEWQI MAY 345	Price OXBEJ MAY 450	Price OEWQG MAY 460	Total Profit/ Loss per Contract	Percent Return
4/13/2009		$402.95	$1.85	$2.25	$1.80	$1.25		
5/16/2009		<=$335	$0	$10	$0	$0		
	Profit/ Loss		$(1.85)	$(7.75)	$1.80	$(1.25)	$(9.05)	(100%)
5/16/2009		$344.05	$0	$0.95	$0	$0		
	Profit/ Loss		$(1.85)	$1.30	$1.80	$(1.25)	$0.00	0%
5/16/2009		$344.60	$0	$0.40	$0	$0		
	Profit/ Loss		$(1.85)	$1.85	$1.80	$(1.25)	$0.55	6.1%
5/16/2009		$345 to $450	$0.00	$0.00	$0.00	$0.00		
	Profit/ Loss		$(1.85)	$2.25	$1.80	$(1.25)	$0.95	10.5%
5/16/2009		$450.55	$0.00	$0.00	$0.55	$0.00		
	Profit/ Loss		$(1.85)	$2.25	$1.25	$(1.25)	$0.40	4.4%
5/16/2009		$450.95	$0.00	$0.00	$0.95	$0.00		
			$(1.85)	$2.25	$0.85	$(1.25)	$0.00	0%
5/16/2009		>=$460	$0.00	$0.00	$10.00	$0.00		
	Profit/ Loss	$(1.85)	$2.25	$(8.20)	$(1.25)		$(9.05)	(100%)

The distribution of the actual stock market has fatter tails and a narrower, more focused distribution about the mean than a Gaussian distribution.

The fat tails of the actual stock market's distribution indicates the stock market experiences large movements more frequently than predicted by the Gaussian distribution. Additionally, the narrow focus of the actual stock market about the mean indicates the stock market exhibits smaller movements on average than as predicted by the

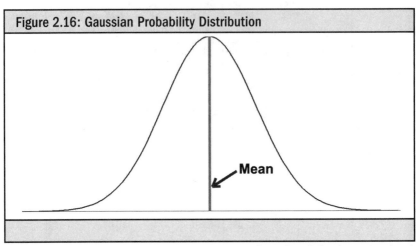

Figure 2.16: Gaussian Probability Distribution

Mean

Source: PowerOptions (www.poweropt.com)

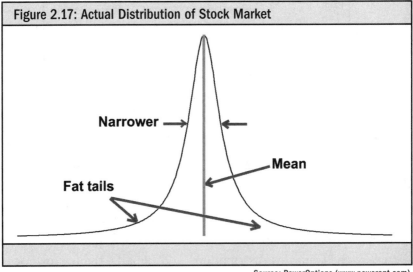

Figure 2.17: Actual Distribution of Stock Market

Narrower

Mean

Fat tails

Source: PowerOptions (www.poweropt.com)

Gaussian distribution. Based on this, the market has a tendency to make very large unexpected movements, and also has periods where it basically does nothing but tread water.

The famous Black-Scholes option pricing model developed by Fischer Black and Myron Scholes was derived based on the assumption that the stock market behaves with a Gaussian distribution. Many, if not most, stock option probability calculations use the Black-Scholes option pricing model, which means the probability calculations based on Black-Scholes have some inaccuracies. For stock options where the price of the underlying equity is close to the strike price of the option, the probability calculations based on the Black-Scholes model are fairly accurate; however, for stock options where the price of the underlying equity is significantly different from the strike price of the option, the theoretical probability calculations developed using Black-Scholes are somewhat less than accurate. The inaccuracies of the Black-Scholes model for the underlying equity price significantly different than the stock option strike price presents problems using the Black-Scholes model for the iron condor strategy.

Consider the OEX index with a price of $439.82 on June 5, 2009 and the previously mentioned call option OXBFN (JUN 470). The number of days to expiration for the call option is 15. A Gaussian distribution-based pricing model shows a theoretical probability of only 2 percent that OEX will be trading above the call option's strike price of $470 at expiration. The calculation using a Gaussian distribution for the theoretical probability that OEX will be greater than the strike price of $470 at expiration is 2 percent; however, using a histogram approach for prices of OEX over the previous year and calculating the theoretical probability yields a 5 percent theoretical probability that OEX will be greater than the $470 strike price at expiration.

The histogram approach exhibits a significantly higher theoretical probability that OEX will be greater than $470 at option expiration than the theoretical calculation using a Gaussian distribution, as illustrated in Table 2.7. The 2 percent versus 5 percent discrepancy between the histogram and Gaussian calculations illustrates nicely the fat tails concept behavior of the stock market. Based on historical data, the price of OEX is 3 percent (5 percent-2 percent) more likely to be above $470 at expiration than as calculated using the model based on a Gaussian distribution.

Table 2.7: Comparison of Black-Scholes versus Histogram

Gaussian Distribution Theoretical Probability OEX Greater than $470 at Expiration	Histogram Theoretical Probability OEX Greater than $470 at Expiration
2%	5%

When determining the theoretical price of an option, the Black-Scholes model has similar negative issues, as it is a Gaussian-based probability calculation. At this point, a reader might ask, "Why doesn't someone develop a more accurate option pricing model?" Other option pricing models have been developed: Binomial, Jump-Diffusion, Markovian, Stochastic, etc. Yet, each alternative option pricing model also has flaws and inaccuracies. Although the Black-Scholes options pricing model has some inaccuracies, it is the only one that has a closed-form solution with relatively good accuracy and that also provides efficient implementation.

PowerOptions uses the Black-Scholes calculation for its tools because of the efficiency of the method. When performing millions of calculations, it is imperative to execute the calculations very expeditiously, even at the cost of some inaccuracies.

To perform the alternative method for calculating options probabilities using historical data, a histogram of an equity's stock price is developed over a certain time period. The histogram of actual price movements can then be used for calculating theoretical option probabilities. This approach considers the actual probability distribution of the underlying over the time period for consideration. The drawbacks to this method are a requirement for a significant number of calculations to be performed for each equity under consideration, and the model may be inaccurate going forward if the sentiment of the market or the underlying has changed.

For example, consider the bull-put credit spread example illustrated previously. The theoretical probability of success based on Black-Scholes was calculated as 93.2 percent. Using a histogram approach over the previous 52 weeks, a probability of success was calculated to be 83.3 percent. Additionally, for the bear-call credit spread example, the Black-Scholes probability of success was calculated as 85.7 percent. Using a 52-week histogram approach, the probability of success was determined to be 98 percent. The comparisons between the Black-Scholes and the histogram calculations are shown in Table 2.8.

Table 2.8: Comparison of Black-Scholes with Histogram Probability of Success

Option Position	Black-Scholes Probability of Success	Histogram Probability of Success
Bull-Put Credit Spread	93.2%	83.3%
Bear-Call Credit Spread	85.7%	98%

As illustrated in Table 2.8, the histogram method was more pessimistic for the bull-put position than the Black-Scholes method, and conversely the histogram method was more optimistic for the bear-call.

For iron condor positions, the accuracy of the Black-Scholes options model must be taken into consideration, since a large number of "interesting" iron condor positions have stock options a significant distance away from the price of the underlying equity. For iron condors, the wider the profitability region of the position or the larger the distance between the short options, the less accurate a Black-Scholes-based theoretical probability calculation is.

To calculate the theoretical probability of success for the iron condor, the probability of success of the bull-put credit spread position and the theoretical probability of success of the bear-call credit spread position are to be taken into consideration. The probability of success for the iron condor is determined by the price of the underlying being between the short option strike prices at expiration, also commonly referred to as the *percent probability between*. The theoretical probability of the bull-put or the bear-call being unsuccessful is calculated as the theoretical probability of success subtracted from the total probabilities of the strategy (100 percent). The equation for calculating the probability of success for an iron condor is:

Probability of Success: Iron Condor

= 100% - [Probability of Unsuccessful Bull-Put + Probability of Unsuccessful Bear-Call]

= 100% - [(100% – Probability of Success Bull-Put) + (100% – Probability of Success Bear-Call)]

In the previous bull-put credit spread example, the Black-Scholes probability of success was 93.2 percent and the Black-Scholes probability of success for the bear-call credit spread example was 85.7 percent. The Black-Scholes probability of success for an iron condor with these positions would be 78.9 percent and calculated as:

$$100\% - [(100\% - 93.2\%) + (100\% - 85.7\%)] =$$
$$100\% - [(6.8\%) + (14.3\%)] =$$
$$100\% - 21.1 =$$
$$78.9\%.$$

The 78.9 percent represents the probability that the underlying is between the short option strike prices at option expiration.

For this example, the creation of the iron condor position through the combination of the bull-put and bear-call positions, and in conjunction with special margin, provided a doubling of the maximum potential return. Typically, an investor would expect to see the theoretical probability of success significantly impacted. Yet, in doubling the return, the Black-Scholes theoretical probability of success of the iron condor has only been slightly impacted, as illustrated in Table 2.9.

Table 2.9: Success versus Return Comparison

Strategy	Theoretical Probability of Success - Black Scholes	Theoretical Probability of Success - Histogram	Maximum Potential Return
Bull-Put Credit Spread	93.2%	83.3%	4.17%
Bear-Call Credit Spread	85.7%	98%	5.82%
Iron Condor	78.9%	83.7%	10.5%

It is interesting to note the implementation of the 52-week histogram method for the iron condor provided a theoretical probability of success of 83.7 percent. Based on the histogram calculation, the iron condor position could be entered with approximately the same amount of risk as the bull-put position by itself. Using the histogram method, an investor considering the bull-put position alone could invest in the iron condor instead—and basically double the estimated return while incurring approximately the same amount of risk.

In general, the higher the theoretical probability of success, the lower the maximum potential return for an iron condor, and conversely, the lower the probability of success, the higher the maximum potential return. A chart illustrating the relationship for potential return versus probability of success for real-world OEX index iron condors with two weeks to expiration is shown in Figure 2.18.

As can be seen in Figure 2.18, for a probability of success greater than 80 percent, the potential returns are 5 percent or less. For probability of success around 70 percent, the potential returns range from 5 percent to 20 percent and for probabilities of success of less than 60 percent, the potential returns range from 20 percent to 55 percent.

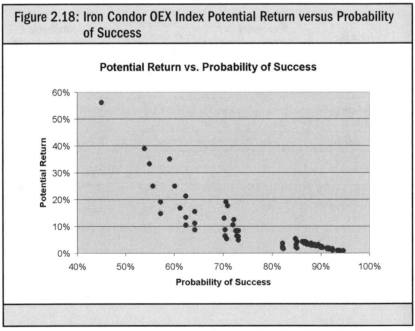

Figure 2.18: Iron Condor OEX Index Potential Return versus Probability of Success

Source: PowerOptions (www.poweropt.com)

The potential returns for iron condors are essentially capped. Iron condors can be rolled to increase potential return, but for the most part, their returns are set at initial entry. An iron condor position with a very high potential risk should have a correspondingly high potential return; however, the return is capped. Even though the position may become more risky after initial entry, the position retains the potential return as when entered.

REVIEW QUESTIONS FOR CHAPTER 2

1. Entry of an iron condor consists of:

    A. Selling two call options and buying two call options

    B. Selling two put options and buying two put options

    C. Selling two short options and buying two long options

    D. None of the above

2. Iron condors are profitable at expiration if:

    A. Underlying security price is between the long options

    B. Underlying security price is between the short options

    C. Underlying security price is between short put options and long put options

    D. None of the above

3. An iron condor consists of:

    A. Bull-put credit spread and bear-call credit spread

    B. Bear-put credit spread and bull-call credit spread

    C. Bull-put credit spread and bear-call debit spread

    D. Bull-put debit spread and bear-call debit spread

    E. None of the above

4. A bull-put credit spread performs best when the underlying is:

    A. Neutral-to-bearish

    B. Neutral-to-bullish

    C. None of the above

5. A bear-call credit spread performs best when the underlying is:

A. Neutral-to-bearish

B. Neutral-to-bullish

C. None of the above

6. Margin requirement for bull-put credit spread is calculated:

A. Short Put Option Strike - Underlying Security

B. [(Short Put Option Strike - Long Put Option Strike) - Bull-Put Net Credit]*100

C. (Short Put Option Strike - Long Put Option Strike)

D. None of the above

7. Typically, iron condor special margin considerations require that:

A. The difference between put spread and call spread be the same

B. Option expirations be in the same month

C. All of the above

D. None of the above

8. The Black-Scholes option pricing model is most accurate for:

A. In-the-money (ITM) options

B. Out-of-the-money (OTM) options

C. At-the-money (ATM) options

D. None of the above

9. A bull-put credit spread with a short put option strike price of $400, a long put option strike price of $390, and an initial net credit of $0.50 would have a margin requirement of:

A. $95

B. $950

C. $1,000

D. $1,050

E. None of the above

10. The maximum potential return for a bull-put credit spread with an initial net credit of $100 and a margin requirement of $1,900 is:

A. 0.53%

B. 5.3%

C. 53%

D. None of the above

11. The maximum potential return for an iron condor *without* special margin consisting of a bull-put net credit of $150 and margin requirement of $1,850 and a bear-call net credit of $250 and margin requirement of $1,750 would be:

A. 1.1%

B. 11.1%

C. 111.1%

D. None of the above

12. The maximum potential return for an iron condor with special margin consisting of a bull-put net credit of $80 and margin requirement of $1,920, and a bear-call net credit of $80 and a margin requirement of $1,920 would be:

A. 4.2%

B. 8.3%

C. 42%

D. 83%

E. None of the above

 Go to the Traders' Library Education Corner at www.traderslibrary.com/TLEcorner for answers to these self-test questions.

Chapter 3

SELECTING THE RIGHT SECURITY

In general, individual stocks are too volatile for an iron condor strategy. The potential for either a large increase or decrease in stock price, resulting in a large loss, is too great for the iron condor strategy to be applied to individual stocks. Poor earnings or an early earnings warning can send a stock plummeting or, conversely, a positive company conference call can propel a stock through the stratosphere. Either scenario spells disaster for an iron condor. For example, consider the stock price of Human Genome Sciences (HGSI) illustrated in Figure 3.1.

Human Genome Sciences reported good news for a clinical trial of a drug in development and the stock skyrocketed, jumping from $3.22 on July 17, 2009 to $12.51 on July 20, 2009. Any iron condor for HGSI with a respectable return entered just prior to July 20, 2009 would have resulted in a total loss of invested capital.

At a minimum, an investor desiring to enter iron condor positions for individual stocks should stick with very large companies, as they are less likely to merge or be acquired. Companies merging or being

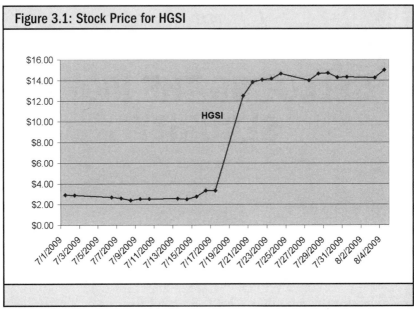

Figure 3.1: Stock Price for HGSI

HGSI

Source: PowerOptions (www.poweropt.com)

acquired by another company can cause very erratic movements in the price of a stock and disastrous results for an iron condor position.

An investor dead set on trading iron condor positions for individual stocks should diversify the positions over several stocks in order to reduce risk to the overall portfolio. Alternatively, an investor set on trading spreads on stocks might consider either bullish or bearish spread trades for stocks instead of neutral-biased iron condors. For trending stocks where it would be difficult to trade iron condors, it might be possible to successfully trade bullish or bearish spreads. For example, if a stock is trending higher, then the investor might consider entering a bull-put credit spread for the stock, and if the stock is trending lower, then the investor might consider entering a bear-call credit spread for the stock.

ETFs

Exchange traded funds (ETFs) trade much like stocks and can hold assets like stocks and bonds. ETFs trade at the aggregate price of the underlying assets making up the fund. ETFs typically charge an annual fee of in the range of 0.1 percent to 1 percent. Additionally, many ETFs pay dividends.

Iron condors based on ETFs can be effectively implemented. ETFs avoid some of the major problems with implementing iron condors for individual stocks. ETFs represent an aggregate of stocks, so they are generally less volatile than individual stocks. An event particular to an individual stock in an ETF has less of an impact because the ETF is diversified with other stocks. Investors do not need to be as concerned with diversification, as ETFs automatically provide it.

There are some issues to be considered for ETFs. Generally, the prices of ETFs are managed via stock splits in order to maintain the price within a certain range, usually less than $100. Maintaining the price of an ETF at less than $100 enables a diverse number of investors to participate; however, this increases the costs of implementing an iron condor. For example, to invest $1,000 with the previous OEX example required only one contract. Investing in an ETF with a price less than $100 could require more brokerage commissions and fees, depending on the broker's commission structure.

As an example, an iron condor position for the NDX index selected for PowerOptionsApplied's *Optium* newsletter on June 22, 2009 will be compared with a similar iron condor for the QQQQ ETF selected on the same day. The NDX index and the QQQQ ETF are based on the same stocks and offer similar price movements on a percentage basis. Although not an issue for trading iron condors, it should be noted that the QQQQ ETF can be purchased and pays a dividend, whereas the NDX index cannot be purchased and does not pay a dividend. A comparison of the NDX and QQQQ iron condor positions is shown in Table 3.1.

Table 3.1: Example Comparison of Iron Condor for Index versus ETF

	NDX Index Iron Condor 6/22/2009		QQQQ ETF Iron Condor 6/22/2009	
Underlying Price		$1,426.61		$35.08
Buy to Open Put	NDUSN JUL 1200	$3.45	QAVSB JUL 28	$0.05
Sell to Open Put	NDUSE JUL 1225	$4.40	QAVSD Jul 30	$0.11
Sell to Open Call	NDVGC JUL 1625	$0.65	QQQQGN JUL 40	$0.02
Buy to Open Call	NDVGM APR 1650	$0.48	QQQQGP JUL 42	$0.01
APR 1650	$0.48	QQQGP JUL 42	$0.01	
Net Credit		$1.12		$0.07
# Contracts Required for $10,000 Investment		4		50
Maximum Potential Profit before Commissions		$448		$350
Maximum Potential Return before Commissions		4.7%		3.6%
Up/Down Percent Profitability Region		14%		14%
Brokerage Commissions $10/Trade and $1.50/ Contract		$16		$85
Net Potential Profit after Commissions		$432		$265
Net Potential Return after Commissions		4.5%		2.7%

The NDX position selected for the *Optium* newsletter had a maximum potential return of 4.7 percent versus a slightly lower 3.6 percent return for the QQQQ position. The iron condor position selected for QQQQ had a similar profitability region as the NDX position, with both the NDX and QQQQ iron condor positions exhibiting a profitability region of 14 percent. The profitability region is the range over which the price of the underlying could move up or down and remain profitable.

A $10,000 investment in the NDX position would consist of executing 4 contracts and the same $10,000 investment for QQQQ would involve trading 50 contracts. The difference in the number of contracts is a result of the difference in the price of the "index versus the ETF" and the resulting difference between the short and long option strike prices. The NDX position had a difference between the strikes of $25, whereas the QQQQ position had a difference of only $2.

For this analysis, we'll assume a commission structure of $10 per trade and $1.50 per contract. Brokerage commissions vary significantly from broker to broker, but the commission structure used for this analysis is reasonable.

Based on the commission structure, the NDX position would require a commission of $16; however, due to the larger number of contracts, the QQQQ position would require a significantly higher commission fee of $85.

The net potential return, after considering brokerage commissions for the NDX position, was reduced slightly from 4.7 percent to 4.5 percent, whereas the QQQQ's return was significantly reduced from 3.6 percent to 2.7 percent as a result of the increased required commissions.

Due to the increased brokerage fees and the smaller maximum potential return for the QQQQ over the NDX, the NDX position was significantly more profitable. The NDX position realized an increased profit potential over the QQQQ position with a similar pre-commission risk/reward ratio.

A different brokerage commission structure— for example $20 per trade, and $1.50 per contract for orders of greater than 50 contracts— would have resulted in identical commissions of $20 and, as a result, no difference in profitability would have been experienced related to the commission structure.

This example illustrates how trading iron condors for higher-priced indexes can be more efficient with respect to brokerage fees and commissions. This example also illustrates the importance of considering brokerage commissions when trading with options and especially for iron condors, since they require four different option contracts per position.

Investing with higher-priced indexes does have some downside for investors seeking to invest in an iron condor position with a small amount of capital. The higher-priced indexes generally make options available every $5, whereas the lower-priced ETFs have options available at every $1. The minimum capital which can be invested in a higher-priced index is $500, whereas the minimum capital that can be invested in a lower-priced ETF is $100. This minimum capital investment issue is generally not an issue, as the profit from investing in iron condors with margins of less than $500 can be severely impacted by transaction costs. For example, an iron condor with a $500 margin requirement and a potential return of 5 percent would have a potential profit of $25. A brokerage commission of just $12.50 would eat up half of the potential profit, leaving a net return of 2.5

percent versus the pre-commission potential return of 5 percent. Investments in iron condor positions should be large enough to mitigate the effects of brokerage commissions.

ETF Liquidity

Another issue related to ETFs is liquidity. Some ETFs are lightly traded, as are their related stock options. In general, it is best to avoid securities that are lightly traded because it can be difficult to receive attractive trade executions. Additionally, lightly traded securities can be more difficult to exit than heavily traded securities, and when a stop-loss is encountered for an iron condor, it is imperative to efficiently exit the position to mitigate the loss.

INDEXES

After ruling out stocks and illustrating some of the disadvantages of trading iron condors on ETFs, investors are basically left with entering iron condor positions for indexes. Index values are generally based on the prices of an underlying basket of securities. Indexes provide an attractive conduit for implementing iron condors. Options on many indexes tend to be heavily traded and the prices of many indexes are in a range where an iron condor can be cost-effectively traded.

Table 3.2 illustrates the advantages and disadvantages for iron condors with respect to stocks, ETFs, and indexes.

Indexes and AM Settlement

One issue with index options, which must be carefully considered, is AM settlement. The options on many indexes are settled or determined based on the aggregate market opening price or the price of the first trade of each component of the index on options expiration

Table 3.2: Advantages and Disadvantages of Various Equities for Iron Condors

Equity	Advantages	Disadvantages
Stocks	· Multitude/Variety of Available Selections · Lower Strike Separation	· Difficult to Diversify · Higher Brokerage Fees for Lower Priced Stocks · Highly Volatile · Lower Option Liquidity for Some Stocks
ETFs	· Diversified · Reduced Volatility · No AM Settlement · Lower Strike Separation	· No Special Tax Consideration · Higher Brokerage Fees · Lower Option Liquidity for Some ETFs
Indexes	· Lower Brokerage Fees · Diversified · Reduced Volatility · Special Tax Consideration	· AM Settlement · Higher Strike Separation

day. This method for settlement is known as *AM settlement*. For AM settlement, the value of an index is based upon the opening market price of each stock within the index. Some examples of index options that are AM settled include: NASDAQ 100 Index (NDX), CBOE Volatility Index (VIX), and S&P 500 Index (SPX). The majority of available index options are AM settled; the few that are PM settled are listed in Table 3.3.

A listing of indexes and their respective method of settlement are available at www.PowerOptionsApplied.com/indexes.asp.

Some indexes, like the Russell 2000 for example, contain stocks that are so lightly traded they might not trade until late in the day, or sometimes they might not trade at all on a given day. While the

Table 3.3: PM Settled Index Options

Name	Ticker Symbol	Style
S&P 100 Index	OEX	American
Short-term S&P 100 Index	RZA, RZB, RZD, RZE	American
PHLX Utility Sector Index	UTY	European
PHLX Gold and Silver Sector Index	XAU	American
Computer Technology Index	XCI	American
S&P 100 Index European	XEO	European
Major Market Index	XMI	European
Oil Index	XOI	American

stocks are actually capable of being traded, the options for the index, which contain the stock, are not being traded. This leaves an investor with an iron condor based on an AM settled index in a precarious situation, because it is not possible to exit the iron condor position on expiration day. The last chance an investor has to exit an iron condor for an AM settled index is before the market close on the day prior to options expiration. In general, it is recommended to exit iron condor positions for AM settled indexes the day prior to expiration if the price of the index is close to a stop-loss.

As an illustration of AM settlement, a real world example will be analyzed. Consider an iron condor position as illustrated in Table 3.4.

Table 3.4: Example Iron Condor Position Stop-Loss Scenario

		Open Price 4/16/08	Price on 4/15/08	Price on 4/16/08	Price on 4/17/08	Settle Price 4/18/08
Underlying Security	NDX	1,790.93	1,794.73	1,846.89	1,840.88	1,891.75
Buy to Open Put	NDYPD APR 1675	$0.88	$0.45	$0.25	$0.22	$0.00
Sell to Open Put	NDYPN APR 1700	$1.85	$0.78	$0.26	$0.25	$0.00
Sell to Open Call	NDYDH APR 1875	$1.10	$0.50	$6.85	$2.17	$16.75
Buy to Open Call	NDYDR APR 1900	$0.43	$0.18	$1.80	$0.20	$0.00
Stop-Loss for Put		1,717	1,717	1,717	1,717	1,717
Stop-Loss for Call		1,856	1,856	1,856	1,856	1,856
Net Credit		$1.64				
Profit/Loss if Exit			4.2%	-14.6%	-1.4%	-64.7%
Maximum Potential Return		7.0%				

This iron condor has a very short time period of 3 days until expiration. This position was chosen to illustrate issues of iron condors and AM settlement. An iron condor position of this short time period to expiration is generally discouraged for consideration as a viable investment.

The maximum potential return for this iron condor position is 7 percent. To realize this profit, the price of NDX had to have a settlement price on April 18, 2008, between the short option strike prices of 1,700 and 1,875. Stop-losses of 1 percent (stop-losses are covered in Chapter 5) have been set for the position at $1,717 and $1,856. If the price of NDX drops below $1,717, the bull-put portion of the iron condor will be exited, and if the price rises above $1,856, the bear-call portion of the iron condor will be exited.

One day after entering the position on April 15, 2008, the position could have been exited with a nice profit of 4.2 percent; however, on April 16, 2008, the price of NDX increased significantly to $1,846.89. The position could have been exited on April 16, 2008 with a -14.6 percent loss.

The price of NDX stabilized on the following day, April 17, 2008, and the bear-call portion of the iron condor could have been exited and the loss experienced for the position would have been -1.4 percent.

As of market close on April 17, 2008, the price of NDX had not breached the stop-loss values of $1,700 and $1,875.

On April 18, 2008, NDX opened with a price breaching the stop-loss value of $1,875; however, the options for NDX could not be traded since the NDX is AM settled. The final settlement price for NDX was $1,891.75 and represented a loss on the position of -64.7 percent. Even if NDX had closed later in the day with a price lower than the short strike price of the call option ($1,875), the position would have still sustained a -64.7 percent loss.

Some positions for the PowerOptionsApplied newsletter experienced this same scenario in November 2005 with substantial losses being realized. Following the catastrophe experienced that month, PowerOptionsApplied's advisory newsletter now recommends closing a dangerous short option position with AM settlement the Thursday prior to expiration. In some cases, even if the underlying is several percentage points from the short option, it is recommended to close the position early. For this example, NDX was 1.9 percent less than the short call strike of $1,875, which seems like a comfortable margin, but it wasn't. For NDX, the necessary safety margin would be in the 3 to 5 percent range, depending on market volatility. If the price of the underlying is within a few percentage points of either option's short strike price, it is highly recommended for iron condors with an AM settled index to be closed on the Thursday prior to expiration. Closing a position early is helpful for avoiding losses related to AM settlement.

Losses experienced for iron condors are as statistically likely as market movements in the up or down direction; however, downward movements of the market tend to be significantly more aggressive than upward movements. Negative news tends to propel a market downward for a larger percentage than the percentage positive news propels a market upward. This knowledge is important for determining whether to exit a position early for AM settlement. For example, an iron condor with potential for transgressing the lower put option short strike price should be given higher consideration for early exit for AM settlement than an iron condor with potential for transgressing the upper call option short strike price.

INDEX TAX ADVANTAGES

Trading broad-based index options for taxable accounts can have some favorable consequences when paying federal income taxes. The IRS has a provision known as Section 1256 Contracts Marked to Market. A section 1256 contract is any regulated futures contract, foreign currency contract, non-equity option, dealer equity option, or dealer securities futures contract.

Broad-Based Index Options

The non-equity option included in the list for Section 1256 is of interest for trading iron condors. The IRS defines a non-equity option as "any listed option that is not an equity option." According to the IRS, non-stock options include debt options, commodity futures options, currency options, and broad-based stock index options. A broad-based stock index is based upon the value of a group of diversified stocks or securities (10 or more). Standard and Poor's 500 index is one example of a broad-based stock index.

60/40 Rule

Generally, capital gains from stock or stock option investments held less than one year are considered short-term, and those held longer than one year are considered long-term; however, according to the IRS, under the marked to market system, 60 percent of a capital gain or loss may be treated as a long-term capital gain or loss and 40 percent may be treated as a short-term capital gain or loss, even if the position was held for less than a year. The ramification of this rule is that capital gains or losses considered to be long-term have lower marginal tax rates than short-term capital gains or losses, and index options for broad-based indexes qualifying under the 60/40 rule have a more favorable tax treatment over options on equities considered short-term investments. Table 3.5 illustrates the 60/40 rule.

Table 3.5: IRS Section 1256 Contracts Marked to Market 60/40 Rule

Long–Term Capital Gain	Short–Term Capital Gain
60%	40%

Tax Savings Example

For example, for a short-term capital gain with a marginal tax rate of 35 percent, the marginal taxes on a $1,000 capital gain would be $350, and for a long-term capital gain with a marginal tax rate of 15 percent, the marginal taxes on $1,000 would be $150.

Using the 60/40 rule, 60 percent of the capital gain, $600, would be taxed at 15 percent and 40 percent of the capital gain, $400, would be taxed at 35 percent, so the taxes paid under the 60/40 rule would be $90 for the portion considered long-term and $140 for the portion considered short-term, for a total of $230, which is $120 less than if the total capital gain were considered short-term. The composite marginal tax rate for this example of the 60/40 rule is 23 percent, 12 percent less than the 35 percent rate for short-term capital gains, and represents paying 34 percent less in income taxes. Table 3.6 illustrates the difference in taxes paid via the 60/40 rule for index options versus the conventional amount of taxes paid.

Table 3.6: Comparison of Taxes for Stock versus Broad Based Index

	Stock, ETF, Narrow Based Indexes	Broad Based Indexes
Tax Consideration	Short-Term Top Marginal Tax Rate	Section 1256 60/40 Rule
Capital Gain	$1,000	$1,000
Tax	$350	$230
Effective Tax Rate	35%	23%

No Tax Advantage for ETFs

As of the writing of this book, it is unclear whether iron condors for broad-based ETFs can be considered for Section 1256 Contracts

Marked to Market. Using the literal definition of an equity option, a broad-based ETF does not appear to qualify for Section 1256.

INDEXES, ETFS, AND STOCKS

In general, we recommend iron condor positions based on indexes, as they provide cost efficiencies for trading, provide tax advantages in certain cases, and are not as prone to large price movements as individual stocks. Although, great care must be taken for iron condors having AM settled options in order to prevent large losses from occurring on expiration days, as previously mentioned.

Iron condors based on ETFs is an acceptable strategy, but it is not as cost efficient as an index-based strategy and is not applicable for Section 1256 tax advantages.

Iron condors for individual stocks are highly discouraged, as individual stocks are subject to large price movements. A portfolio of iron condor positions for individual stocks however, can be a viable strategy.

AMERICAN VERSUS EUROPEAN

Another important issue to consider is the style of an option. Options basically come in two flavors: American and European. The purchaser of an option can exercise an American style option at any time, but a European style option can only be exercised on the option's expiration date.

Generally, American versus European style options is not a significant issue to consider as iron condor positions generally consist of out-of-the-money options, which are seldom exercised early.

If an option for an iron condor position transitions to in-the-money, or even close to in-the-money, the investor must be cognizant that the option can be exercised. If the option exercised is a call option, it can be called away. If the option is a put option, it can be "put" to the investor.

Early exercise of an option for an iron condor position can result in a loss on the position and can require immediate action for managing the position in order to prevent an additional loss.

In general, European style index options are not in danger of being exercised; however, ETFs and stocks are generally American-style options and can be exercised at any time by the purchaser of the option. Hence, European style index-based iron condor positions have an advantage over stocks and ETFs because they cannot be exercised early and do not require management of a position as a result of the options being exercised.

The majority of index options are European style. The few that are American style are listed in Table 3.7.

Table 3.7: American Style Index Options

Name	Ticker Symbol	Settlement
S&P 100 Index	OEX	PM
Short-term S&P 100 Index	RZA, RZB, RZD, RZE	PM
PHLX Semiconductor Sector Index	SOX	AM
PHLX Gold and Silver Sector Index	XAU	PM
Computer Technology Index	XCI	PM
Oil Index	XOI	PM

A listing of index options with their respective style is available at www.PowerOptionsApplied.com/indexes.asp.

REVIEW QUESTIONS FOR CHAPTER 3

1. Iron condors may receive special tax considerations for:

   A. Stocks

   B. ETFs

   C. Broad-based indexes

   D. None of the above

2. Iron condor traders with a position consisting of options for an underlying index should beware of:

   A. AM settlement

   B. PM settlement

   C. All of the above

   D. None of the above

3. Iron condor traders have additional management considerations for options that are:

   A. American style

   B. European style

   C. All of the above

   D. None of the above

4. Commissions for iron condors are lower for securities that are:

   A. Lower in price

   B. Higher in price

   C. None of the above

5. For the 60/40 rule:

   A. 60% of capital gain or loss is considered short-term and 40% long-term

   B. 60% of capital gain or loss is considered long-term and 40% short-term

   C. Invest 60% in iron condors and 40% in other investments

6. The most difficult securities for implementing successful iron condors are:

   A. Indexes

   B. ETFs

   C. Individual stocks

   D. Bonds

 Go to the Traders' Library Education Corner at www.traderslibrary.com/TLEcorner for answers to these self-test questions.

Chapter 4

FINDING SUCCESSFUL IRON CONDORS TO TRADE

BROKERS

There are a host of brokers available for trading iron condors. Here is a sample listing of brokers.

- charlesSCHWAB

- Fidelity

- Interactive Brokers

- Investrade

- tradeMONSTER

- optionshouse

- optionsXpress

- thinkorswim

- TradeKing

- zecco

Areas of consideration for selecting a broker for option trading are:

- trading requirements;

- brokerage fees and commissions—including special spread commissions;

- margin considerations;

- order execution capability and efficiency—including contingent stop-order capability;

- analysis tools, technical and trading support; and

- other intangibles.

TRADING REQUIREMENTS

Brokers have varying minimum capital requirements for trading stock options. Before opening an account intended for iron condor trading, an investor should verify that the broker will allow option trading for the amount of capital to be placed in the account. Some brokers allow investing with iron condors in individual retirement accounts (IRAs) and some do not. An investor seeking to trade this strategy in an IRA account should verify with the broker of choice to make sure iron condor trading is allowed in an IRA. Additionally, brokers may have requirements based on a trader's experience level before allowing the customer to trade options.

BROKERAGE FEES AND COMMISSIONS

Brokerage fees and commissions are a very important consideration when selecting a broker, as this can significantly impact the profitability of the iron condor strategy. Brokerage fees vary significantly between brokers depending on the size of the trading account and the number of transactions executed per month or per year. Additionally, the trade execution method for the iron condor strategy must be considered, as brokerage fees will vary depending on whether the strategy is executed as a four-leg spread option trade, as two two-leg spread option trades, or four single option trades. In general, the fees for implementing an iron condor will be less if the position can be entered and rolled as a four-leg spread trade.

MARGIN CONSIDERATION

Some brokers do not allow for special margin considerations for iron condors, which negatively impacts the return for the iron condor strategy.

ORDER EXECUTION

Iron condor traders will desire the capability to enter spread trades with a parameter for Net Credit/Limit. Net Credit/Limit capability enables traders to enter trades between the aggregate bid and ask for the position, potentially improving the strategy's potential return.

Contingent orders based on the price of the underlying equity are another capability iron condor traders will seek. Contingent orders enable option investors to configure their trades to be automatically executed in the event that a stop-loss is encountered. As of the writing of this book, optionsXpress and tradeMONSTER are known to provide contingent orders based on the price of the underlying equity.

Iron condor investors will require fast and efficient execution of positions in order to maximize potential returns and limit losses. A potentially lucrative iron condor position can disappear very quickly, so it is crucial for brokers to place trades efficiently. Additionally, a position not exited in a timely manner as a result of a stop-loss can incur a significantly larger loss than a position closed very quickly.

ANALYSIS TOOLS

The tools available to option traders vary widely across option brokers. Generally, two million potential iron condor trades are available for entry at any given point in time. Option tools enable the large number of iron condor possibilities to be reduced to a small number of plausible trades tailored specifically for the risk/reward profile of the particular investor. Investors should carefully investigate and evaluate brokers and third-party option tools, like PowerOptions, for trading iron condors.

INTANGIBLES

Iron condor traders will desire brokers geared for option trading. The degree of technical and trading support offered by the various brokers varies significantly. Some brokers offer online technical and trading support via Internet chat. The web site interface provided by some brokers is intuitive and easy to use, while other web site interfaces are unwieldy and difficult to use. Some brokers are geared specifically for option traders and offer excellent support for trading options, while others are geared more for other types of trades, such as stocks, commodities, etc., and provide token support for option traders.

Investors new to option trading would be best served to select a broker providing the best amenities, albeit with higher trading costs and less profit, than to go with a low-cost broker. An inexperienced trader could sustain a significant loss as a result of attempting to trade with a low-cost broker rather than going with a broker offering higher tier services with higher costs. After gaining experience with the higher tier broker, an option trader might consider transitioning to a lower cost broker for increased potential profit, but with less support.

Investors new to options might also consider an advisory newsletter service, like PowerOptionsApplied. A newsletter service enables options traders to learn from an expert, which can aid in avoiding costly mistakes.

SELECTING SUCCESSFUL IRON CONDORS

Selection of successful iron condors is primarily based on balancing the behavior of the underlying equity, expected return, average expected loss, stop-loss settings, and theoretical probability of success. Table 4.1 illustrates the balancing act for finding successful iron condors.

Table 4.1: Iron Condor Return Scenarios

Initial Expected Return	Average Expected Loss	Theoretical Probability of Success	Stop-Loss % Margin	Annualized Expected Return
3%	20%	90%	0%	8%
5%	25%	85%	0%	6%
7%	30%	80%	0%	-5%
10%	40%	75%	0%	-30%
3%	10%	85%	1%	13%
5%	12%	80%	1%	19%
7%	15%	75%	1%	18%
10%	20%	70%	1%	12%

The return scenarios illustrated in Table 4.1 are partially based on hypothetical and partially based on historical trading of index–based iron condors over the 2005 to 2009 time frame.

As you can see, unless stop-loss margin is utilized, the iron condor strategy consistently has low returns or generates a loss. The larger the initial expected return without a stop-loss, the less the annualized return, or the larger the annualized loss.

By simply implementing a 1 percent stop-loss margin, the annualized results of trading the iron condor are significantly improved. The stop-loss margin for this example is defined as exiting an iron condor position when the price of the underlying equity is within a price distance of less than 1 percent of either of the strike prices for the sold options as, illustrated in Figure 4.1.

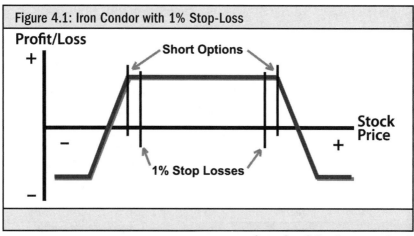

Figure 4.1: Iron Condor with 1% Stop-Loss

Source: PowerOptions (www.poweropt.com)

The equations for calculating the stop-loss values are:

Put Stop-Loss = Short Put Strike Price * (1+%Stop-Loss)
Call Stop-Loss = Short Call Strike Price * (1-%Stop-Loss)

As can be seen from Table 4.1, increasing the initial expected return can actually have a negative impact on the annualized expected returns, whereas the sweet spot for the scenario is with 1 percent stop-losses and with initial expected returns in the 5 to 7 percent range.

The probabilities of experiencing stop-losses increase significantly as potential returns are increased and the losses experienced also increase significantly as a result of increased potential returns.

For positions with higher potential profit, the combination of the increased number of stop-losses experienced with the increased size of the losses creates a condition in which it is difficult for profitable positions to overcome the frequency and size of the losses.

UNDERSTANDING THE PAST FOR MAKING PROFIT IN THE FUTURE

Even though the results listed in Table 4.1 are partially based on historical trading results, the results of Table 4.1 are not an indication of future results. Analysis of the past can be useful for making better decisions in the future. A graph of the following components is illustrated in Figure 4.2.

- CBOE Volatility Index (VIX)
- SPDR S&P 500 Index ETF (SPY)
- major market events
- stop-losses experienced by the PowerOptionsApplied Meridian TradeFolioTM
- percent up/down profitability region for Meridian's SPX/OEX iron condor positions

The time period for Figure 4.2 is from December 2006 through June 2009. The market events illustrated in Figure 4.2 are listed in Table 4.2.

Table 4.2: Market Events Illustrated in Figure 4.2

Date	Market Event
4/2006	Housing bubble pop
6/22/2007	Bear Stearns hedge fund busted
3/17/2008	Bear Stearns merger
9/8/2008	Fannie Mae and Freddie Mac placed into conservatorship by U.S. Government
9/15/2008	Bankruptcy of Lehman Brothers

All of the market events listed had specific dates as to their occurrence except for the housing bubble pop. The housing market started to unravel in approximately April of 2006 for some parts of the United States, but the full culmination of the housing bubble's demise transpired over the course of many months.

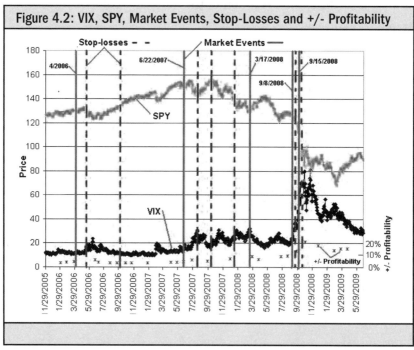

Figure 4.2: VIX, SPY, Market Events, Stop-Losses and +/- Profitability

Source: PowerOptions (www.poweropt.com)

The PowerOptionsApplied *Meridian TradeFolio™* typically enters iron condor trades expecting to return between 2 and 4 percent per month. The trades are entered for broad based indexes and stop-losses are set in the range of 1 to 2 percent of the short option strike prices. The positions are entered the week following options expiration and are entered for an expiration time of typically one month. Generally, the index options for *Meridian* expire worthless with the investor retaining the initial net credit as profit. The positions are not rolled and the offending short and long options are exited very quickly after experiencing a stop-loss condition.

For the VIX, as illustrated in Figure 4.2, the higher the value observed, the higher the volatility of the market. The VIX is a popular measure of the implied volatility of S&P 500 index options.

The SPY, also shown in Figure 4.2, is an ETF, which tracks the performance of the S&P 500. The S&P 500 is a value-weighted index of 500 large capitalization common stocks traded in the United States.

As illustrated in Figure 4.2 and enumerated in Table 4.3, four extended time periods of greater than four months were experienced for the *Meridian Iron Condor TradeFolio™* where no stop-losses were experienced.

Table 4.3: Extended Time Periods Without Stop-Loss for Meridian Iron Condor TradeFolio™

Time Period	# Months Without Stop-Loss	Market Event and Volatility Spike Just Prior
June 2006 to Oct. 2006	5	Yes
Nov. 2006 to Aug. 2007	10	No
Jan. 2008 to July 2008	7	Yes
Oct. 2008 to June 2009	9	Yes

In every extended time period without a stop-loss, except one, a market event and a spike in volatility preceded the run of successful iron condor trades. In each time period of successful iron condors, the market volatility trend following the initial spike was generally lower. The outlier case where a profitability run occurred without experiencing a market event or spike in volatility occurred following the June 2006 to October 2006 run of successful positions and could be considered a continuation of the June 2006 to October 2006 string of successful trades. Another way to look at it would be as experiencing a time period of 15 months from June 2006 to August 2007 with only one stop-loss after the market event and volatility spike of April and May of 2006.

A situation to consider for Figure 4.2 is the time period from June of 2007 to March 2008. During this time, a market event and volatility spike was experienced, but was not followed by successful trades. Rather, it was followed by several stop-losses. The difference between this time period of unsuccessful trades and the successful ones listed in Table 4.3 is the behavior of the VIX. For the successful cases of Table 4.3, the VIX immediately started to drop after the initial spike; however, for the time period of June 2007 to March 2008, the VIX did not immediately fall in value, but rather remained elevated and experienced additional spikes following the initial spike.

One last element to be gleaned from Figure 4.2 is the up/down profitability range with respect to volatility. The up/down profitability range indicates the amount the underlying equity can increase or decrease in price before experiencing a stop-loss. As illustrated in Figure 4.2, a 4 percent up/down profitability range is typically experienced for an OEX/SPX position for *Meridian*. Additionally, as observed in Figure 4.2, the up/down profitability range potential increases with increased volatility and vice-versa. In October 2008, market volatility jumped significantly and iron condor positions for *Meridian* experienced up/down profitability values in the 20 percent range. This means iron condor positions available would have been profitable as long as the underlying equity did not increase or decrease more than 20 percent after entry.

Based on the previous analysis and discussion, it is best to enter iron condor positions following a market event and volatility spike with the volatility quickly falling and trending lower after the initial spike. A rule of thumb for determining a volatility spike after which an iron condor position might be entered is a value for the VIX of greater than 20.

An illustration confirming the usefulness of this rule of thumb can be observed in Figure 4.2 following the Bear Stearns merger on March 17, 2008 and continuing until the Fannie Mae and Freddie Mac takeover on September 8, 2008. Prior to the Bear Stearns merger, the value of VIX had fallen near or below the value of 20. The value of the VIX spiked above 30 at the announcement of the Bear Stearns merger on March 17, 2008. The VIX immediately began to drop following the merger and continued in a general downward direction until the Fannie Mae and Freddie Mac event on September 8, 2008 caused the VIX to spike upward. Between the two VIX spikes caused by Bear Stearns and Fannie Mae and Freddie Mac, the *Meridian TradeFolio*™ had a sustained six-month time period of profitability.

Successful trading of iron condors in future markets will require pertinent variables to be analyzed based on current market conditions. For example, a trader may need to increase or decrease the initial expected return based on market volatility. Generally, iron condors with higher initial expected returns can be entered in markets with higher volatility following a market event.

Iron condor investors can also anticipate average expected losses to be higher in markets with higher volatility. In higher volatility markets following a market event, the probabilities of success for an iron condor will be higher, all else being equal. In more volatile markets, iron condor positions will generally require larger stop-loss margins. In volatile markets, iron condor positions can also generate higher annualized returns, all else being equal. Successful future trading of iron condors also requires the analysis of underlying equities for attractiveness. Iron condor investors must evaluate the prospects for the underlying, whether it is expected to trend up, trend down, or trend sideways, and whether the volatility will increase, decrease, or stagnate. Variables to consider with respect to market volatility are illustrated in Table 4.4.

Table 4.4: Variables and Market Volatility Following a Market Event

Variable	Low Relative Market Volatility	High Relative Market Volatility Following a Market Event
Initial Expected Return	Less	Greater
Average Expected Losses	Less	Greater
Theoretical Probabilities of Success	Less	Greater
Stop-Loss Values Required	Smaller	Larger
Annualized Returns	Less	Greater

TIME VALUE AND TIME TO EXPIRATION

In general, it is recommended to trade shorter lifespan iron condors in the range of two to five weeks to expiration to take advantage of increased time value decay. The closer a stock option is to expiration, the faster the time value decays, which increases the average annualized return, all else being equal. An illustration of an option's time value decay is shown in Figure 4.3.

As can be seen from Figure 4.3, the time value of a stock option decays in a fairly linear fashion in the first 600 days, begins to exponentially decay over the following 280 days, and rapidly decays in its final 20 days.

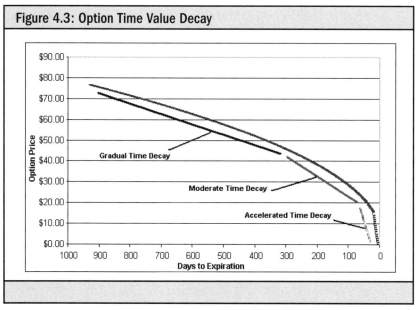

Figure 4.3: Option Time Value Decay

Source: PowerOptions (www.poweropt.com)

BID–ASK SPREADS

The options for an iron condor often have large bid–ask spreads, as the options can be significantly out-of-the-money. In general, it is recommended to avoid spreads with very large bid–ask differentials because it can cause a larger loss if the position has to be exited as a result of a stop-loss.

To maximize potential return when entering an iron condor position, it is recommended to initially enter the positions via net limit orders and to use the midway point between each option's bid–ask to spread determine the value for the net limit order.

For example, consider the bull-put credit spread position illustrated in Chapter 2. The market price for the bull-put would have been the ask price of $1.85 for the purchased put option, subtracted from the sold put option's bid price of $2.25, for a net credit of $0.40. The midway point between the bid and ask for the long put option was $1.50+($1.85-$1.50)/2, or $1.68, and the midway point between the bid and ask for the short put option was $2.25+($2.65-$2.25)/2, or $2.45.

The midway point between bid and ask net credit would be $2.45-$1.68, or $0.77, almost double the market net credit of $0.40. It is very common to achieve execution using a net credit limit with the midway point between bid and ask values, and for this particular example, the maximum potential return for the bull-put was almost doubled. A comparison of using market versus midway point between the bid and the ask for the bull-put position is shown in Table 4.5.

Table 4.5: Comparison of Market and Midway Point Between Bid/Ask for Bull-Put

OEX @ $402.95 on 4/13/2009	Market	Midway Point Between Bid/Ask
Long Put OEWQG (MAY 335)	$(1.85)	$(1.68)
Short Put OEWQI (MAY 345)	$2.25	$2.45
Net Credit	$0.40	$0.77
Maximum Potential Return	4.17%	8.34%

Performing the same calculation for the bear-call credit spread of Chapter 2, the midway point between bid and ask net credit is calculated to be $0.88 calculated as shown here.

$$[\$1.80+(\$2.10-\$1.80)/2] - [\$0.90+(\$1.25-\$0.90)/2] =$$
$$[\$1.80+(\$0.30)/2] - [\$0.90+(\$0.35)/2] =$$
$$[\$1.95] - [\$1.07] =$$
$$\$0.88$$

This represents an almost 50 percent improvement over the market net credit of $0.55. A comparison of using market versus midway point between the bid and the ask for the bear-call position is shown in Table 4.6.

Table 4.6: Comparison of Market and Midway Point Between Bid/Ask for Bear-Call

OEX @ $402.95 on 4/13/2009	Market	Midway Point Between Bid/Ask
Long Call OXBEL (MAY 460)	$(1.25)	$(1.07)
Short Call OXBEJ (MAY 450)	$1.80	$1.95
Net Credit	$0.55	$0.88
Maximum Potential Return	4.17%	9.65%

Performing the maximum potential return for the iron condor using the net credit of $0.77 for the bull-put and $0.88 for the bear-call results in a maximum potential return of 19.8 percent, or almost double the return using the market prices for the stock options. A comparison of the return calculations using market and midway points between bid and ask is shown in Table 4.7.

Table 4.7: Comparison of Market Return versus Midway Point Between Bid/Ask

Position	Return with Market	Return with Midway Point Between Bid/Ask
Bull-Put Credit Spread	4.17%	8.34%
Bear-Call Credit Spread	5.82%	9.65%
Iron Condor	10.5%	19.8%

FINDING A POSITION

Finding an iron condor position can be a daunting task, as there can be almost two million iron condor positions to choose from at any point in time. A search tool, like PowerOptions for example, can significantly decrease the effort required to find suitable iron condor positions since positions can be screened based on relevant parameters in real time.

Important parameters iron condor investors will desire to limit for a search are:

- Probability of Success/Probability Between;

- Potential Return;

- Equal Margin for Bull-Put and Bear-Call Spreads;

- Universe of Equities Searched;

- Total Net Credit;

- Option Open Interest;

- Spread Separation/Maximum Risk; and

- Expiration Month/Days to Expiration.

PROBABILITY OF SUCCESS

One of the most important parameters for successful iron condor investing is the *probability of success,* or the probability that the underlying is expected to be between the short option strike prices at option expiration. Investors seeking to invest in iron condors will need the capability to restrict the number of positions considered based on the probability of success. Since losses incurred from exiting a position as a result of a stop-loss can be fairly large, it is important to optimize the aggregate return over time by balancing the number of stop-losses experienced, the percent loss sustained for stop-losses, and the return for successful positions.

Limiting searched positions to ones with a high probability of success enables investors to enter positions likely to succeed based on past history. Typically, investors will want to limit potential iron condor investments to ones with a probability of success greater than 85 percent.

POTENTIAL RETURN

An investor might consider this parameter unnecessary. He might think after limiting the available positions to those with the highest probability of success, that simply choosing a position with the highest potential return out of those would be the best strategy. But, high potential returns can also lead to large losses as a result of exiting a position due to a stop-loss.

Positions with high potential returns possess long options with significant value, so if a stop-loss is incurred, the long options must be immediately closed to prevent an additional loss. Long options with significant value impede the capability to recover from the initial loss by leaving the long option or a portion of the long option open. This also limits the capability for using a long option to hedge against other iron condor portfolio positions sustaining a loss. As a rule of thumb, iron condor positions based on indexes should be limited to maximum potential returns of no greater than 9 percent. Above potential returns of 9 percent, the potential for risk far outweighs the potential for return.

EQUAL MARGIN FOR BULL-PUT AND BEAR-CALL SPREADS

Critical to iron condor investing is the ability to limit positions to those with an equal spread for the bull-put and bear-call portions of the iron condor. This enables investors to take advantage of special margin provided by some brokers. The ability to invest in iron condors with special margin can significantly increase the returns experienced over positions not qualifying for special margin. To take advantage of special margin, investors must be able to find positions with equal spreads.

UNIVERSE OF EQUITIES SEARCHED

Since investing in stock-based iron condors requires significant risk, investors will desire to restrict the securities that can be considered primarily to indexes and ETFs. Additionally, iron condor investors sensitive to tax considerations may want to further limit the universe of search to broad-based indexes in order to take advantage of IRS section 1256.

TOTAL NET CREDIT

Investors may seek to limit the minimum total net credit for an iron condor position in order to prevent returns from being negatively impacted by transaction costs. For example, consider an iron condor with a total net credit of $0.05. The $0.05 total net credit represents a profit before expenses of $5 per contract. At $5 profit per contract, brokerage commissions and fees can significantly impact the net returns. For this example, an average transaction cost of greater than $5 per contract would result in a guaranteed loss on the position. To reduce the impact of commissions and fees on net return, an iron condor investor would generally want to limit searches to positions with a net credit of greater than $0.25.

OPTION OPEN INTEREST

Option open interest is an important parameter to consider for iron condors, as it is important to efficiently exit a position in the event of a stop-loss hit. The more open interest for an option, the more likely an order for the option will be executed in a timely and cost-efficient manner. An option with low option interest could take a prolonged time to execute and also could be executed at an exorbitant price. At a minimum, the open interest for each option of an iron condor should be greater than 100.

SPREAD SEPARATION/MAXIMUM RISK

Investors in iron condors will want to control the spread between the short and long options. This separation minus the initial net credit is commonly referred to as *maximum risk*, as it represents the maximum risk per underlying. Narrow spreads generally result in smaller losses in the event of a stop-loss; however, narrower spreads also incur larger transaction costs because more contracts are required to enter a position than with wider spreads. Conversely, wider spreads tend to incur larger losses as a result of stop-losses, but require less brokerage fees and commissions. For iron condors based on indexes, it is generally best to maintain a spread between 4 and 26.

EXPIRATION MONTH/DAYS TO EXPIRATION

Iron condor investors will seek to limit the time frame of an investment. Iron condors perform best in shorter time frames, generally in the range of 10 to 40 days to expiration. Longer time frame iron condors are more likely to sustain a loss than shorter time frame positions. Additionally, the loss as a result of hitting a stop-loss for a longer time frame iron condor will be larger than for a trade with shorter time-frame. The time frame of an iron condor can be limited by selecting the month of expiration, the days to expiration, or a combination of expiration month and days to expiration.

An example of a search tool provided by PowerOptions for iron condors is shown in Figure 4.4.

Figure 4.4: Example Iron Condor Search Tool

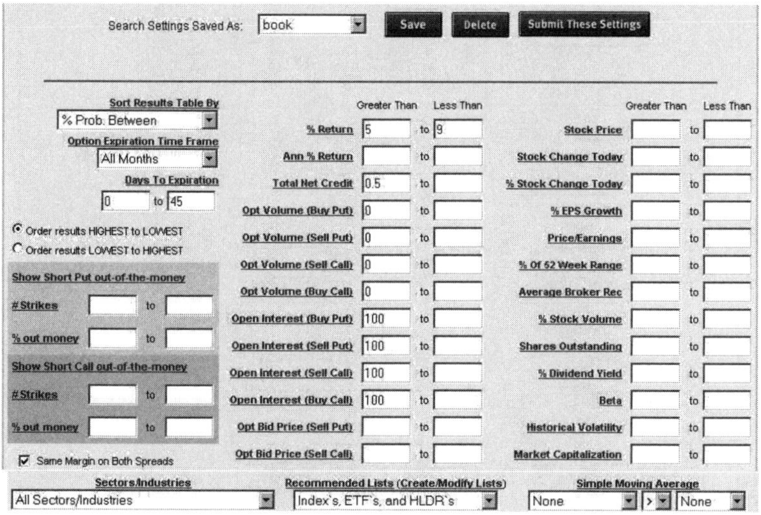

Source: PowerOptions (www.poweropt.com)

As you can see, the search tool enables an investor to select various parameters to find a suitable position. The PowerOptions search tool provides all the necessary parameters for finding iron condors: probability of success, potential return, equal margin, universe of equities, total net credit, option open interest, maximum risk, and expiration time frame.

More Info	Stock Sym	Last Stock Price & Chg	Exp Date	Buy Put Ask	Buy Put Strike	Sell Put Bid	Sell Put Strike	Sell Call Bid	Sell Call Strike	Buy Call Ask	Buy Call Strike	Lower Break Even	Upper Break Even	Total Net Credit	% Return	% Prob Between
	$NDX	1,634.12 (+28.14)	SEP 19 2009	0.55	1,375.0	0.70	1,400.0	2.35	1,715.0	1.15	1,740.0	1,398.65	1,716.35	1.35	5.7	89.6
	$RUT	566.14 (+3.65)	OCT 17 2009	1.15	420.0	1.50	440.0	1.40	640.0	0.65	660.0	438.90	641.10	1.10	5.8	88.7
	$RUT	566.14 (+3.65)	OCT 17 2009	1.40	430.0	1.50	440.0	1.40	640.0	0.95	650.0	439.45	640.55	0.55	5.8	88.5
	$NDX	1,634.12 (+28.14)	SEP 19 2009	1.00	1,425.0	1.15	1,450.0	2.35	1,715.0	1.15	1,740.0	1,448.65	1,716.35	1.35	5.7	88.2
	$RUT	566.14 (+3.65)	OCT 17 2009	1.40	430.0	1.80	450.0	1.40	640.0	0.65	660.0	448.85	641.15	1.15	6.1	87.8
	$NDX	1,634.12 (+28.14)	OCT 17 2009	3.20	1,300.0	3.40	1,325.0	3.80	1,800.0	2.70	1,825.0	1,323.70	1,801.30	1.30	5.5	87.7
	$RUT	566.14 (+3.65)	OCT 17 2009	1.65	440.0	1.80	450.0	1.40	640.0	0.95	650.0	449.40	640.60	0.60	6.4	87.5
	$RUT	566.14 (+3.65)	OCT 17 2009	2.00	450.0	2.70	470.0	0.80	650.0	0.45	670.0	468.95	651.05	1.05	5.5	87.4
	$RUT	566.14 (+3.65)	OCT 17 2009	0.85	400.0	1.05	420.0	2.25	630.0	0.95	650.0	418.50	631.50	1.50	8.1	87.2
	$NDX	1,634.12 (+28.14)	SEP 19 2009	1.35	1,450.0	1.50	1,475.0	2.35	1,715.0	1.15	1,740.0	1,473.65	1,716.35	1.35	5.7	87.1

Additionally, the PowerOptions search tool provides other parameters for tailoring positions for specific fundamental and technical data. The PowerOptions search tool also provides the capability to search for positions using real-time data that can be crucial for efficient trade execution. The PowerOptions search tool supports many different strategies—other than the iron condor—that aid investors with diversifying their investments. It is important for iron condor investors to not only diversify their investments by security, but also by strategy, and PowerOptions' tools will be very beneficial in this area.

The results found for the set of search parameters in Figure 4.4 yielded the iron condor positions shown in Figure 4.5.

The search returned several positions with potential returns ranging from 5 to 9 percent and with probabilities of success based on the Black-Scholes option pricing model greater than 85 percent. The patented PowerOptions SmartSearchXL tool provides the capability to adjust the return parameter, theoretical probability of success, range OTM, and many other criteria to allow investors to find only those positions matching their personal risk-reward profile. An investor seeking to sacrifice return for a higher probability position could lower the potential return range 3 to 5 percent and increase the probability of success parameter to greater than 90 percent, for example.

ENTERING A POSITION

A convenient method for entering an iron condor position is via a four-leg trade entry screen provided by most brokers. The PowerOptions search tool provides one-click trade entry for selected brokers via its BrokerLink utility. For example, by selecting an iron condor position from a PowerOptions search result for a BrokerLink trade, the screen shown in Figure 4.6 is made available.

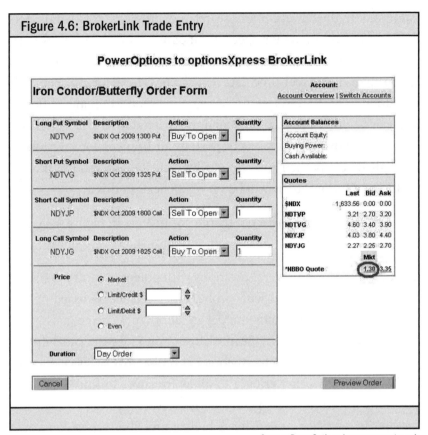

Figure 4.6: BrokerLink Trade Entry

PowerOptions to optionsXpress BrokerLink

Iron Condor/Butterfly Order Form

Account:
Account Overview | Switch Accounts

Long Put Symbol	Description	Action	Quantity
NDTVP	$NDX Oct 2009 1300 Put	Buy To Open ▾	1

Short Put Symbol	Description	Action	Quantity
NDTVG	$NDX Oct 2009 1325 Put	Sell To Open ▾	1

Short Call Symbol	Description	Action	Quantity
NDYJP	$NDX Oct 2009 1800 Call	Sell To Open ▾	1

Long Call Symbol	Description	Action	Quantity
NDYJG	$NDX Oct 2009 1825 Call	Buy To Open ▾	1

Price
○ Market
○ Limit/Credit $
○ Limit/Debit $
○ Even

Duration: Day Order ▾

Account Balances
Account Equity:
Buying Power:
Cash Available:

Quotes

	Last	Bid	Ask
$NDX	1,633.56	0.00	0.00
NDTVP	3.21	2.70	3.20
NDTVG	4.60	3.40	3.90
NDYJP	4.03	3.80	4.40
NDYJG	2.27	2.25	2.70
			Mkt
*NBBO Quote		1.30	3.35

Cancel

Preview Order

Source: PowerOptions (www.poweropt.com)

For entry of an iron condor position, the long put and call options should be designated as "Buy to Open," and the short put and short call options should be designated as "Sell to Open," as illustrated in Figure 4.6.

In general, the quantity of the number of contracts should be identical for each stock option traded. The investor has the option of selecting the trade for "Day Order" or "Good Until Cancelled." For a Day Order, the broker will only make the trade available for the current day. For Good Until Cancelled, the broker will make the trade available until the investor cancels the order.

As shown in Figure 4.6, the market net credit is $1.30 and the maximum potential market return is calculated to be 5.5 percent. The net credit for the midpoint of the bid–ask spread is determined to be $2.33 and is calculated as shown below.

$$\{[3.4+(3.9-3.4)/2] - [2.7+(3.2-2.7)/2]\} + \{[3.8+(4.4-3.8)/2] - [2.25+(2.7-2.25)/2]\}=$$
$$\{[3.4+(0.50)/2] - [2.7+(0.50)/2]\} + \{[3.8+(0.60)/2] - [2.25+(0.45)/2]\} =$$
$$\{[3.65] - [2.95]\} + \{[4.10] - [2.47]\} =$$
$$\{\$0.70\} + \{\$1.63\}=$$
$$\$2.33$$

The maximum potential return is calculated to be 10.3 percent using the midpoint between the bid–ask spread, which is significantly greater than the market return of 5.5 percent. A comparison of market versus using midway point between the bid–ask spread is shown in Table 4.8.

Table 4.8: Comparison of Market and Midway Point Between Bid–Ask

NDX @ 1633.56 on 9/4/2009	Market	Midway Point Between Bid–Ask
Long Put NDTVP (OCT 1300)	$(3.20)	$(2.95)
Short Put NDTVG (OCT 1325)	$3.40	$3.65
Short Call NDYJP (OCT 1800)	$3.80	$4.10
Long Call NDYJG (OCT 1825)	$(2.70)	$(2.47)
Net Credit	$1.30	$2.33
Maximum Potential Return	5.5%	10.3%

A trader could enter the position as a market order, or with a Limit/Credit of $1.30 and almost be guaranteed order execution with a resulting maximum potential return of 5.5 percent. More advantageously, an investor could enter the trade using the Limit/Credit for the midpoint of the bid–ask, $2.33, and there is a good chance the trade would execute resulting in a maximum potential return of 10.3 percent, almost twice the potential return using market prices.

A trader entering the position with the midpoint between bid–ask Limit/Credit of $2.33 and experiencing non-execution of the entry could gradually lower the Limit/Credit value until the trade executes. Small movements in the underlying will have little effect on the net credit, which can be received.

For example, an increase in the price of the underlying will decrease the net credit received for the bull-put. This decrease, however, will be compensated for, thanks to an increase in the net credit received for the bear-call. A reverse of this situation occurs when the price of the underlying decreases in price, with the bull-put net credit increasing and compensating for a decrease in the bear-call net credit.

Entering iron condor trades with bid–ask midpoint Limit/Credit may require more effort to execute, but the extra income generated is well worth it.

After selecting and executing iron condor trades, it is important to monitor positions for rolling and stop-loss conditions. An example of a tool for monitoring positions is the PowerOptions Portfolio Tool. PowerOptions' Portfolio Tool enables traders the capability to monitor important parameters like an iron condor's current aggregate profit/loss, individual option profit/loss, and days to expiration. A screenshot of the NDX position after entry into PowerOptions Portfolio Tool is shown in Figure 4.7.

Figure 4.7: Example Portfolio Tool for Monitoring Positions

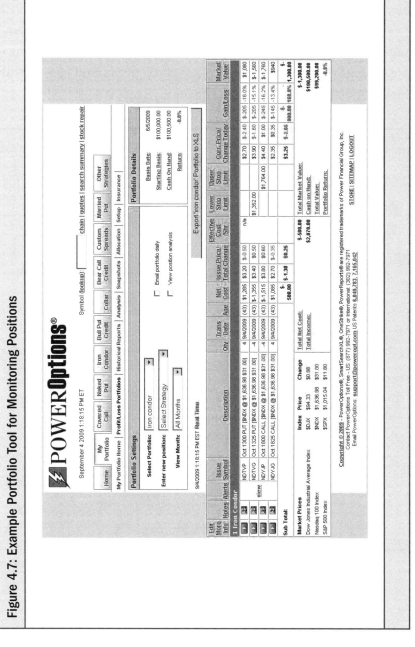

Source: PowerOptions (www.poweropt.com)

PowerOptions Portfolio Tool enables investors to monitor and set alerts for their positions for a variety of conditions: stock price, stock percent change, option bid, option ask, option percent change, moving averages, Bollinger Bands, and 52–week high and low. An example screenshot of the alerts, which can be set for an iron condor with PowerOptions Portfolio Tool, is shown in Figure 4.8.

Figure 4.8: PowerOptions Alerts for Iron Condor

Leg #2: Sell 4 contracts of NDTVG (OCT 09 1,325.00 PUT) @ $3.40			Current Bid/Ask: $3.30 / $3.90	
Enabled	Alert Type	Alert Criteria		
☑	Stock Price Limit	Lower Limit: 1352	Upper Limit:	
☐	Stock % Change	% Decrease:	% Increase:	
☐	Option Ask Limit	Lower Limit:	Upper Limit:	
☑	Option % Change	% Decrease: 80	% Increase:	

Leg #3: Sell 4 contracts of NDYJP (OCT 09 1,800.00 CALL) @ $3.80			Current Bid/Ask: $4.00 / $4.50	
Enabled	Alert Type	Alert Criteria		
☑	Stock Price Limit	Lower Limit:	Upper Limit: 1764	
☐	Stock % Change	% Decrease:	% Increase:	
☐	Option Ask Limit	Lower Limit:	Upper Limit:	
☑	Option % Change	% Decrease: 80	% Increase:	

Position Alert Settings

Enabled	Alert Type	Alert Criteria		
☐	Position % Change	% Decrease:	% Increase:	

Underlying Alert Settings

Enabled	Alert Type	Alert Criteria		
☐	SMA #1	Stock Price	<	SMA 20
☐	SMA #2	Stock Price	<	SMA 20
☐	Lower Bollinger Band	Stock Price	<	Lower Band 20
☐	Upper Bollinger Band	Stock Price	<	Upper Band 20
☐	52 Week Low	Stock Price	<	52 Week Low
☐	52 Week High	Stock Price	<	52 Week High

Source: PowerOptions (www.poweropt.com)

LEGGING–IN TO A POSITION

Another trade entry option available to investors is legging-in to an iron condor position. Legging-in to an iron condor can generate positions with relatively wide profitability regions at the expense of additional brokerage commissions. The wide profitability regions generated using this method are a result of entering spread positions contrary to the movement of the market. The additional brokerage commissions are a result of having to pay for two trade entries for two spread positions instead of paying for a single four-leg spread trade. For some brokers, the commission for a four-leg iron condor trade is often cheaper than for two two-leg spread trades.

For this scenario, an investor would initially enter either the bull-put credit spread or the bear-call credit spread, followed by the later entry of the remaining spread position. Entry of a bull-put or bear-call position is similar to the entry of an iron condor, except an investor uses a two-leg order entry page instead of a four-leg entry page.

In general, the legging-in strategy involves entering a bear-call position when the market is rallying and entering the bull-put position when the market is retreating. A potential drawback to this strategy is that in the case of a solidly bearish or bullish market, an investor may not have an opportunity to enter both positions and may end up with only one spread position. There is a good chance the one spread position will experience a loss and there will be few opportunities for recovering the loss because a second spread position wasn't entered to aid in mitigating a loss.

SEPARATION BETWEEN SOLD AND PURCHASED STOCK OPTION

The separation between the sold and purchased options for a spread must be considered. A large separation is more economical to trade than a small separation, as the number of options required for a large separation is less than what is required for a small separation, even for the identical amount of capital invested. For example, for a 10-point separation between sold and purchased options, each contract entered represents $1,000 of capital invested, and for a 5-point separation, each contract represents $500 of capital invested, as illustrated in Figure 4.9.

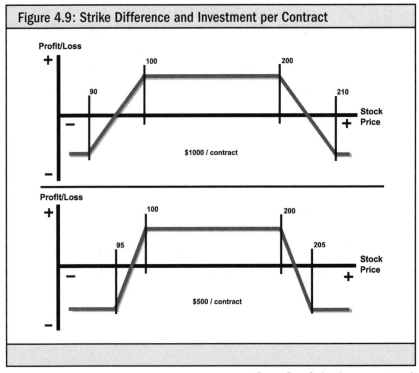

Figure 4.9: Strike Difference and Investment per Contract

Source: PowerOptions (www.poweropt.com)

For this example, a $1,000 investment and a 10-point strike difference would require 1 contract, and the 5-point spread, for the same $1,000 investment, would require 2 contracts. The 5-point strike difference could incur twice the amount of brokerage fees, depending on the broker's commission, as compared to the 10-point strike difference structure.

The drawback to a larger separation between sold and purchased options is that as the separation between the options becomes larger, the more the long option is out-of-the-money and the larger the distance between the bid and ask prices. The larger the bid and ask prices for the long option, the more difficult it is to exit the position efficiently in the event of a stop-loss, for example. Additionally, for small separations between the sold and purchased stock options, it can be difficult to find a position within the desired range of the maximum expected return.

The drawback to a smaller separation between sold and purchased options is the potential for a large loss related to AM settlement. The smaller the separation between the sold and purchased options, the more likely an underlying equity will move significantly in-the-money at market open on the Friday of options expiration and result in a large loss.

For capital investments in increments of $5000, it is possible to invest the same amount of capital by adjusting the number of contracts whether the position consists of a 1-, 5-, 10- or 25-point spread.With identical amounts of capital invested, the maximum potential loss with the varied point spreads is also identical.

For PM settled equities, it is generally best to select an iron condor position with the minimum short/long spread possible, which also meets the desired capital requirement, the potential return requirement, and the budget for brokerage commissions. This provides a position with the minimum risk related to stop-loss and there is no associated risk related to AM settlement. For AM settled equities, it is best to select a short/long spread, which reduces the potential for a loss related to AM settlement and also does not incur a large loss from hitting a stop-loss. For AM settled indexes, a short/long spread in the range of 10 to 25 usually presents a good trade-off between AM settlement risk and stop-loss risk.

IMPORTANT CONCEPTS FROM THIS CHAPTER

- A suitable broker for trading iron condors should be selected.

- Broker support for contingent orders for exiting iron condors is advantageous.

- Capability to search for and find appropriate iron condors based on a set of criteria is a plus.

- For iron condor index trades, it is advisable to set stop-losses at least 1 percent away from the short option's strike.

- Iron condors on indexes with potential returns in the 5 to 7 percent range tend to have optimal attractive risk–reward ratios.

- It is best to enter iron condors after a major market event and with market volatility trending lower.

- Selection of iron condor positions and related stop-losses should be considered in light of current market conditions.

- Iron condor positions that expire within 2 to 5 weeks of entry should be chosen.

- Entering iron condor trades at the midway between the bid and ask option prices can achieve significant additional potential return over market prices.

- Investing in iron condors which qualify for special margin can double potential return.

- For iron condors based on indexes, it is generally best to find positions with a spread between the short and long options of between 4 and 26.

- Iron condors should be entered using a four-leg order entry in order to receive attractive net credits and economical brokerage commissions.

- It is advantageous for iron condor traders to have a method for being alerted when an iron condor trade needs management.

REVIEW QUESTIONS FOR CHAPTER 4

1. The most important thing for a rookie to consider when selecting a broker for options trading is:

    A. Brokerage fees and commissions

    B. Support

    C. Good looking web site

    D. None of the above

2. Finding successful iron condors requires consideration of the:

    A. Behavior of the underlying equity

    B. Expected return

    C. Average expected loss

    D. Stop-loss settings

    E. All of the above

3. Time-value decays fastest for iron condors that are:

    A. Closest to expiration

    B. Furthest from expiration

    C. None of the above

4. The best returns for iron condors are received for orders entered for:

    A. Market prices

    B. Between bid and ask prices

    C. Between bid and market prices

    D. Between ask and market prices

    E. None of the above

5. The best search method for finding iron condors is:

   A. Reading *The Wall Street Journal*

   B. Asking your friends

   C. PowerOptions

   D. Broker's option chain

   E. None of the above

6. The most efficient and profitable method for entering an iron condor trade is:

   A. Two-leg market order

   B. Four-leg market order

   C. Four-leg limit/credit order

   D. Four-leg market order

   E. None of the above

 Go to the Traders' Library Education Corner at www.traderslibrary.com/TLEcorner for answers to these self-test questions.

Chapter 5

MANAGEMENT OF IRON CONDORS

The management of iron condors must be considered prior to entering the positions. Determining management decisions prior to entry of a position provides an environment in which:

- Decisions can be made in an unemotional and logical manner;

- Time constraints are not an issue;

- Second-guessing is avoided, and;

- Correct choices are made for management of positions.

Many factors must be considered prior to entering an iron condor including:

- Stop-losses;

- Expected return;

- Market volatility;

- Capital outlay;

- Capital reserve;

- Rolling;

- Diversification, and;

- Early exit.

Prior to entry of iron condor positions, a trader must make decisions related to the early exit of the positions. Additionally, traders must stick with their plan for early exit, or face the consequences of a potentially large loss.

Actual results will depend heavily on iron condor management decisions. The higher the expected returns, the more management required, and the higher potential for sustaining larger losses. Stop-loss margins that are too small can contribute to sustaining larger losses. Conversely, stop-loss margins that are too large can require unnecessary exits with increased management and decreased profits. The more diversified a portfolio of iron condors, the less the impact incurred as a result of a stop-loss for one position.

Additionally, the more diversified a position is, the less capital reserve required per position for exiting in the event of a stop-loss. Iron condors with larger percentage capital outlays must be handled very carefully in order to prevent a catastrophic loss of capital. All of these factors must be considered prior to entry in order to experience successful and profitable trading of iron condors.

STOP-LOSSES

A stop-loss is a predetermined exit point. If a stop-loss condition is met at any point during market hours, the iron condor position is modified in some manner. In general, it is recommended to set predetermined stop-loss points for managing an iron condor.

A stop-loss does not guarantee that a position will be exited at the predetermined price. For example, an underlying equity may make a sudden upward or downward move at market open and jump past the stop-loss point. Sudden market movements propelling an underlying equity past a stop-loss point can cause significant losses for iron condors. This is the primary reason it is not recommended to trade iron condors based on stocks, as stocks are more likely to make very large movements than indexes or ETFs.

Stop-loss settings should be dynamic based upon market conditions, especially related to volatility. The higher the volatility, the larger the stop-loss margins should be. Conversely, a market with low volatility should have lower stop-loss margins. A common stop-loss set point for iron condors is when the underlying moves within 1 percent of either of the short option strike prices. The calculations for determining the values for the stop-losses were illustrated in Chapter 4. For the previously mentioned bull-put position, a 1 percent stop-loss for the short put option strike price of 345 would be set at 348.5, 1 percent higher than the strike price. For the bear-call example, a 1 percent stop-loss would be set at 445.5 or 1 percent below the short call strike price of 450. The calculations for 1 percent stop-losses (as discussed in Chapter 4) are:

$$\text{Put Stop-Loss} = 345 * (1 + 1\%)$$
$$= 345 * (1 + 0.01)$$
$$= 348.5$$

$$\text{Call Stop-Loss} = 450 * (1 - 1\%)$$
$$= 450 * (1 - 0.01)$$
$$= 445.5$$

A profit and loss diagram illustrating a 1 percent stop-loss is shown in Figure 5.1.

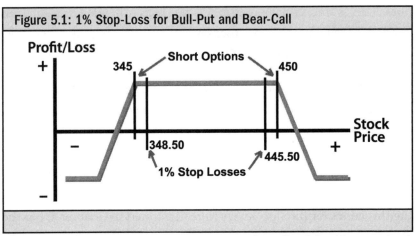

Figure 5.1: 1% Stop-Loss for Bull-Put and Bear-Call

Source: PowerOptions (www.poweropt.com)

The benefit of stop-losses will be illustrated with a real world example from PowerOptionsApplied's *Optium* newsletter. An iron condor for the *Optium* newsletter was entered for the NDX index on November 2, 2005 with a maximum potential return of 8.9 percent, as illustrated in Table 5.1.

Upper and lower stop-losses were set at $1,632 and $1,513, respectively. The stop-loss settings represented 1 percent of the short option strike prices.

On November 4, 2005, when the NDX was close to breaching the upper stop-loss of $1,632, the stop-loss was modified slightly from $1,632 to $1,636 with hopes the market would retrace. The stop-loss was modified only slightly, as we had only been in the position for three days. A larger modification of the stop-loss would have made the position vulnerable to a very large loss.

Table 5.1: Example Iron Condor Position Stop-Loss

		Open Price 11/2/05	Stop-Loss modify on 11/4/05	Price at Stop-Loss 11/8/05	Expected profit / loss at expiration as of 11/8/05	Expected profit / loss at expiration on 11/25/05 if had not used stop-loss
Underlying Security	NDX	$1,581	$1,631.79	$1,636.84		$1,691.09
Buy to Open Put	NDTWT NOV 1475	$1.35				$(1.35)
Sell to Open Put	NDVWJ NOV 1500	$2.20				$2.20
Sell to Open Call	NDVKM NOV 1650	$2.15		$7.90	$(5.75)	$(38.94)
Buy to Open Call	NDVKD NOV 1675	$0.95		$1.35	$0.40	$15.14
Stop-Loss for Put	$1,513		$1,513			
Stop-Loss for Call	$1,632		$1,636			
Net Credit		$2.05			$(4.50)	$(22.95)
Maximum Potential Return		8.9%			-19.6%	-100%

The NDX index did not retrace as expected and the revised upper stop-loss of $1,636 was breached on November 8, 2005. The bear-call spread position was closed and the position realized a loss of -19.6 percent at expiration on November 25, 2005.

To see the importance of setting and adhering to stop-losses for iron condor positions, we will analyze what would have happened if the stop-losses had not been set or were ignored.

At expiration on November 25, 2005, the NDX index settled AM at a price of $1,691.09, which was higher than the short call strike price of $1,650 and the long call strike price of $1,675. As illustrated in Table 5.1, not exiting the position with a proper stop-loss would have incurred a total loss of the initial margin requirement.

It is possible for an iron condor investor to experience a loss of -20 percent and recover from the loss; however, it doesn't take very many total losses on iron condor positions to reach a point of no return and be in a position of not being able to recover from the dramatic loss of capital. Stop-losses are not a guarantee of iron condor investing success, but they do significantly increase the probability of success.

In hindsight, the initial position entered for *Optium* was too aggressive, with a maximum potential return of 8.9 percent. In recent years, the maximum potential returns of *Optium* have been more in the range of 6 to 8 percent, which is more of a sweet spot for success with iron condors. For example, Optium averaged a 6 percent monthly return for 2009 with a success rate of 100 percent.

CLOSING SHORT AND LONG OPTIONS OR CLOSING ONLY SHORT OPTIONS

A common strategy for iron condor stop-losses is to exit short options, which are in a precarious condition. For example, if the price of the underlying is within a certain percentage, typically 1 percent of the short strike price of the sold option, then the offending sold options would be closed and the related long options would remain open.

The idea behind leaving the long options open is the hope or expectation of the underlying equity continuing to move toward the open long options. With a continued movement of the underlying in the direction of the open long option, the loss, which occurred as a result of closing the short option, might be ameliorated or recovered. The key for success is determining whether the underlying will continue to move in the direction of the open long option or perform a retrace.

The drawback to this strategy is in the event the long options possess significant value. Then, a retrace in the underlying could add or compound the loss, as the long options will lose value very quickly as the underlying performs a retrace.

Long options not having a significant value, say less than 2 to 3 percent of the invested capital, can provide a nice hedge if the underlying continues to move toward the open long options. If the underlying continues to move toward the long options, then the position could recoup some of the loss as a result of closing the short options. It is possible the position could even return to profitability if the underlying continues to move in the direction of the open long options. For long options having only a small value when experiencing a stop-loss, a retrace of the underlying would not significantly add to the loss already experienced on the position. In general, it is recommended to close the long options once the position has been restored to profitability. The goal in this situation is to realize a profit, not make a million dollars, as profits can very quickly vanish and turn into a loss with even a small retrace of the underlying.

In most cases, it is recommended to leave the related long options open when the "long option price to capital invested" ratio is less than a few percentage points. If the value of the "related long options to capital invested" ratio is greater than a few percentage points, then it is recommended to immediately close the related long options in order to prevent an additional loss on top of what has already been experienced.

As an example, consider an iron condor position opened on December 24, 2007 for the RUT index with an initial maximum potential return of 7.5 percent, as shown in Table 5.2.

Table 5.2: Example Iron Condor Position Stop-Loss Scenarios

		Open Price 12/24/2007	Price at stop-loss for Put 1/8/2008	Price at close-of-market 1/8/2008	Price at close-of-market 1/9/2008
Underlying Security	RUT	$792	$712	$704.86	$712.12
Buy to Open Put	RUYMR JAN 690	$1	$7	$8.5	$5
Sell to Open Put	RUTMT JAN 700	$1.40	$9		
Sell to Open Call	RUZAL JAN 860	$0.80			
Buy to Open Call	RUZAN JAN 870	$0.50			
Stop-Loss for Put	712				
Stop-Loss for Call	845				
Net Credit		$0.70	$(1.3)	$0.20	$(3.3)
Maximum Potential Return		7.5%	-14%	2.2%	-35%

Immediately closing both long and short put options when the price of RUT touched the stop-loss price of $712 would have incurred a net loss of -14 percent. Closing the short put at the occurrence of the stop-loss and then waiting until the close of market to close the long put would have resulted in a net gain of 2.2 percent; however, closing the short put at the occurrence of the stop-loss and waiting only one day to close the long put would have resulted in a very large net loss of -35 percent.

Management of an open long option must be handled very carefully. The longer the position is open, the larger the potential for experiencing unpleasant negative consequences. Leaving a long option with significant value open for a few minutes or a couple hours to take advantage of a short-term trend is plausible, but leaving a long option with significant value open past the market close is a very dangerous strategy and should be avoided.

As can be seen from Table 5.2, it is very important that an iron condor stop-loss be managed carefully in order to prevent an uncomfortable but palatable stop-loss from turning into a very large and unpleasant stop-loss. Additionally, prudent management of an iron condor stop-loss can result in the recovery of a position, as shown in Table 5.2.

CLOSING SHORT AND PARTIALLY CLOSING LONG

Another stop-loss management strategy is to immediately close the offending short options and close a portion of the offending long options. The remaining open long options are then closed at a later time or date. This is especially prudent if the long options have moderate value, in the range of 5 to 20 percent of margin.

For example, consider a stop-loss condition where the remaining long options have a value of 5 percent of the margin. If the entire long option position was left open after closing the short options and the underlying security retraced in value, then the long options could potentially incur an additional 5 percent loss on top of the loss already experienced.

If, however, half of the long options were closed immediately after experiencing the stop-loss, then the remaining long options only have a value that is 2.5 percent of the value of the margin requirement. In this scenario, the largest additional loss the position could experience with a retrace of the underlying is 2.5 percent, which is more acceptable than experiencing an additional 5 percent loss. If the underlying security continues to move in the direction of the remaining open portion of the long options, then a loss may be reduced or eliminated, or a profit may even be realized.

Let's look at an example from the PowerOptionsApplied *Optium* newsletter of closing a portion of the long option after a stop-loss. An iron condor position was entered on September 18, 2006 for the OEX index with a maximum potential return of 7.5 percent as illustrated in Table 5.3.

Upper and lower stop-losses were set at $624 and $586, respectively. On October 3, 2006, the price of OEX was in danger of breaching the upper stop-loss of $624 and since the position had been in effect for 15 days, it was decided to modify the upper stop-loss; however, since there were 17 days left until expiration, the stop-loss was only modified slightly to $624.30.

On the following day, October 4, 2006, the upper stop-loss was transgressed and the short call options and half of the long call options were immediately closed. If all of the long call options had immediately been closed on October 4, 2006 after experiencing the stop-loss, the position would have experienced a -8.6 percent loss at expiration. The open long call options had significant value, 8.6 percent of margin. Leaving all of the long options open would have left the position vulnerable to a potential loss of -17.2 percent. By closing half of the long option positions, the position was left vulnerable to a loss of only -10.8 percent.

Table 5.3: Example Iron Condor Position—Stop-Loss and Partially Close Long Options vs. Closing All Long Options

		Open Price 9/18/06	Price at Stop-Loss on 10/4/06	Profit/loss at Expiration on 10/20/06 & Closing All Long Call Options on 10/4/06	Price on 10/5/06 & Close Remaining Half Long Call Options	Price on 10/13/06 & Close Remaining Long Call Options – Choice Taken by Optium	Price at Expiration on 10/20/06 & Entire Long Call Options Expire with Zero Value
Underlying Security	OEX	$609	$628		$628.59	$633.61	$636.01
Buy to Open Put	OEBVN OCT 570	$0.85					$0
Sell to Open Put	OEBVP OCT 580	$1.15					$0
Sell to Open Call	OEYIF OCT 630	$0.60	$2.30	$(1.70)			$0
Buy to Open Call	OEYIH OCT 640	$0.20	$0.80	$0.60	$0.90	$0.70	$0
Stop-Loss for Put		$586	$586.00				
Stop-Loss for Call		$624	$624.30				
Net Credit		$0.70		$(0.80)	$(0.75)	$(0.85)	$(1.60)
Maximum Potential Return		7.5%		-8.6%	-8.1%	-9.1%	-17.2%

By closing half the long options, the position was exposed to a small additional loss of -4 percent instead of an additional loss of -8 percent. Additionally, with the open long call options, the trade was in a position to recover from the loss if the price of OEX continued to increase. The remaining call options were left open for nine days until October 13, 2006, after which they were closed. The position eventually suffered a loss of -9.1 percent at expiration.

Three other iron condor positions for SPX, NDX, and RUT were open simultaneously with the OEX position. Two of the positions, RUT and NDX, resulted in profits, and the SPX position sustained a loss. Similar to the OEX iron condor, half of the long options for SPX were left open after experiencing a stop-loss. Unfortunately, after experiencing the stop-losses, the prices of OEX and SPX did not cross the long call option strike prices of $640 and $1,385, respectively, and the aggregate loss for all of the iron condor positions was -1.5 percent for the month.

The optimal time to have closed the remaining open long options was on the day following the stop-loss, October 5, 2006, and the loss would have been recovered slightly, sustaining a -8.1 percent loss. Given the circumstances with the other remaining open profitable positions, the course of action followed was the best choice, even if it meant a slight increase in the loss. If all of the long options had been closed on October 5, 2006 and the market continued to rally, then the open OEX long call options would not have been available as a hedge to protect against a loss for the RUT and NDX positions.

Had the market continued to rally, the two profitable positions, RUT and NDX, would have most likely sustained a loss. The open long call options for OEX and SPX would have acted as a hedge to ameliorate a loss sustained on RUT and NDX. For example, consider the scenario illustrated in Table 5.4.

Table 5.4: Management of Iron Condor Portfolio

Index	Exp. Ret. at Entry	Upper Stop-Loss	Bear-Call Spread Short Call Strike/Long Call Strike	10/4/2006		10/12/2006					
				Act. Price	Exp. Price	Act. Price	Exp. Ret.	% Price Chg from 10/4	Est. Price	Exp. Ret.	Est. % Price Chg from 10/4
OEX	7.5%	624	630 / 640	628	-9.1%	633	-9.1%	0.8%	645	17%	2.7%
NDX	7.3%	1,748	1,775 / 1,800	1,681	7.3%	1,719	7.3%	2.3%	1,812	-15%	7.8%
RUT	7.0%	772	780 / 800	733	7.0%	757	7.0%	3.3%	814	-15%	11.1%
SPX	7.5%	1,361	1,375 / 1,385	1,350	7.5%	1,363	-11.0%	1.0%	1,395	40%	3.3%
Avg. Exp. Ret.	7.3%				3.2%		-1.5%			6.8%	

At initial entry, the expected return for the iron condor portfolio was 7.3 percent. After the stop-loss for the OEX position was experienced on October 4, 2006, the average portfolio expected return was 3.2 percent. Following the SPX stop-loss on October 12, 2006, the average portfolio expected loss was -1.5 percent, which was also the actual loss experienced at expiration.

Suppose the market were to become very bullish following the SPX stop-loss experienced on October 12, 2006 with the OEX, NDX, RUT, and SPX reaching prices of $645, $1,812, $814, and $1,395, respectively. The hypothetical percentage price movements for these indexes are linearly comparable on a percentage basis with price movements experienced from October 4, 2006 to December 12, 2006.

For this hypothetical scenario, the NDX and RUT iron condors sustain stop-losses resulting in expected losses of -15 percent for each. Since the OEX and SPX both had long call options open, the long call options for NDX and RUT would have been immediately closed, as the iron condor portfolio was sufficiently hedged by the open OEX and SPX long call options.

With the bullish move of the market, the open call options for the OEX are now $5 in-the-money, calculated as the strike price of the call option subtracted from the price of the OEX index, or $645-$640. The in-the-money OEX call options result in an estimated expected return of +17 percent. Similarly, the SPX call options are $10 in-the-money, resulting in an estimated expected return of 40 percent. The resulting aggregate average return for all four iron condor positions is now 6.8 percent. Hypothetically, leaving the long call options for the OEX and SPX open after experiencing a stop-loss would have enabled the portfolio of iron condors to generate a profit instead of a loss with a large market movement. Conversely, a large market move in conjunction with *closing* all of the long call options immediately would have resulted in an estimated average expected loss of -12.5 percent.

When trading a portfolio of iron condors, the aggregate risk–reward for the positions must be considered instead of the risk–reward for each individual position. Leaving some long options open after experiencing a stop-loss can result in a profit following a large market movement instead of a loss. Leaving the long options open can result in an additional loss; however, the upside reward is often worth the additional risk.

CONTINGENT STOP-LOSS ORDERS

A convenient method for managing stop-losses for iron condors is via contingent stop-loss orders. A contingent stop-loss order can be entered that will automatically be triggered when the price of the underlying transgresses a stop-loss. Some brokers prove the capability to enter contingent stop-loss orders that will automatically be triggered when the price of the underlying transgresses a stop-loss. After the contingent condition is triggered, a market order will be placed to modify the iron condor position. The contingent order can be configured to close only the short option, or to close the short and long option of the spread position. As of the writing of this book, known brokers supporting contingent stop-loss orders include optionsXpress and tradeMONSTER.

Generally, for investors who are not readily available to manage the long position after encountering a contingent stop-loss order, it is recommended to use a contingent order to close both long and short positions when experiencing a stop-loss.

For investors who are readily available to manage a position after experiencing a stop-loss, contingent orders can be configured to close only the short option. In this case, the investor will be required to determine when to close the remaining long position and will be required to execute the close of the long position manually.

Additionally, investors can configure their account to notify them via email or cell phone text message when a contingent stop-loss order has been triggered. This enables the investor to be notified of a stop-loss condition needing to be managed.

Entering Contingent Stop-Loss

Entering a contingent stop-loss order is fairly straightforward, but an investor must be very careful when entering the polarity of the triggering price, as an incorrect entry can result in the immediate execution of the contingent order.

Two options available for entering contingent stop-loss orders are closing the entire spread, bull-put or bear-call, or closing only the precarious short option.

Closing the entire spread position enables investors to "set and forget." Investors can set the contingent order and be assured the position will be managed without their intervention. Investors implementing this strategy must remember to leave sufficient spare capital in their trading account to allow for closing a worst-case stop-loss condition.

Closing only the precarious short option gives an investor the potential for recovering or partially recovering a loss. For this situation, the short option would be closed via the contingent stop-loss order, and the investor would manage the remaining open long option for the spread.

Two cases are illustrated in Table 5.5.

Table 5.5: Management of Open Long Option After Stop-Loss

Remaining Percent of Capital in Open Long Option After Stop-Loss	<2-3%	>3-4%
Management of Open Long Option	Leave long option open until recover loss or partial loss	Close open long options or portion of long options immediately or before market close

For the case in which the value of the long option is a small percentage of the capital invested in the iron condor, 2 or 3 percent for example, an investor might leave the long option open with the hope that the underlying security will continue to move in the direction of the long option and increase in value. In the event the underlying security retraces or moves away from the long option, the investor will only suffer a small additional loss.

If the value of the long option is a large percentage of the capital investment, greater than 3 or 4 percent for example, the investor should consider closing the long options or closing a portion of the long options immediately after encountering a stop-loss or prior to the close of market on the day the stop-loss was encountered.

As an example, consider the previous iron condor position with a margin requirement of $1,000 per contract and a stop-loss of 1 percent. Suppose a trader experiences a stop-loss at 348.5 for the short put option with the short put option subsequently being closed. Also, suppose the value for one contract of the long put option is $10. This would represent an additional maximum potential loss of 1 percent calculated at $10/$1,000. So for a risk of 1 percent, the position could be hedged against further downside of the equity, as the value of the put option will increase with further downside movements of the underlying. If the underlying increased in price, then the only additional loss would be 1 percent.

Instead, suppose the value for one contract of the long put option is $100. In this case, the additional risk is 10 percent, calculated at $100/$1,000. In this case, the position is hedged against a further drop in the price of the underlying, as in the previous example; however, a retrace or increase in the price of the underlying could result in the loss of an additional 10 percent on top of the loss that had already been sustained with the closing of the short put option.

Failing to close a long option with a significant value can increase the loss for the position if the underlying security retraces or moves away from the open long option.

STOP-LOSS AND CAPITAL REQUIREMENTS

In general, it is recommended to reserve some capital in a trading account to allow for the execution of stop-loss orders for iron condors with special margin. A loss of capital is usually sustained when hitting a stop-loss. If capital has not been reserved in the account, then an iron condor with special margin cannot be exited by simply closing the precarious short option or closing the precarious spread position. This can leave a position in a very dangerous spot and potentially exposed to a very large loss.

To close an iron condor in an account with insufficient capital reserve requires closing the non-precarious spread position, followed by closing the precarious short option or spread position. In general, a capital reserve of 30 percent of the iron condor with the largest margin requirement will be sufficient to allow for managing a portfolio of iron condors in the event of a stop-loss.

For example, in an account with several iron condor positions, suppose the position with the largest capital requirement was $10,000. In this case, a capital reserve of $3,000 would generally be sufficient to manage the stop-loss of the iron condor position. At first glance, this reserve capital requirement would appear to significantly impact the investment return of iron condors. In an account with several iron condors, however, the reserve capital required for the largest iron condor capital requirement would be spread out across several positions. For this to be effective, the positions have to be uncorrelated, or at least not highly correlated. Iron condor positions for several stocks all in the same industry would not be considered uncorrelated.

For example, consider an account with four iron condors with capital requirements of $10,000 each. The recommended capital reserve requirement would be $3,000, so the actual reserve requirement per iron condor would only be $750. In effect, the total capital investment for one $10,000 iron condor would be $13,000, but for four iron condors, would be $10,750 per position—significantly less capital required on average. The additional capital required for stop-loss management dilutes the returns of an iron condor position, as illustrated in Table 5.6.

Table 5.6: Expected Return Considering Reserve Capital

	One Iron Condor	Four Iron Condors
Capital Invested	$10,000	$40,000 (4 @ $10,000)
Expected Return	$1,000	$4,000 (4 @ $1,000)
Account Reserve for Stop-Loss	$3,000	$3,000
Effective Capital Investment	$13,000	$43,000
Effective Return Considering Reserve	7.7%	9.3%

Prior to considering the iron condor stop-loss management reserve requirement, the expected return was 10 percent. However, taking reserve capital into account, the maximum expected return for an account with one iron condor is 7.7 percent versus an account with four iron condors and a maximum expected return of 9.3 percent. Multiple iron condor positions not only diversify the risk, but also reduce the amount of aggregate reserve capital required for stop-loss management.

MODIFYING STOP-LOSSES

Stop-loss settings should be considered dynamic and modified as the situation dictates. Typically, stop-loss margins can be reduced as the iron condor position nears expiration. In general, it is best to refrain from reducing stop-loss margins until the week of expiration. In some cases, stop-losses may need to be increased if the market experiences a sudden increase in volatility. Additionally, the stop-loss margin for iron condor positions with AM settlement may need to be increased on the Thursday prior to expiration in order to prevent a large loss as a result of a large movement in the underlying at Friday's open. As previously mentioned, if an AM settled index option position is in doubt, then it should be closed on the Thursday prior to market close.

Let's review an example of modifying a stop-loss. This example was a position executed by the PowerOptionsApplied *Optium* newsletter, which was entered on January 27, 2007 for the RUT index. Table 5.7 illustrates the initial position, the modification of the stop-loss values, and the profit/loss for the position.

Table 5.7: Example Iron Condor Stop-Loss Modification

		Open Price 1/27/07	Price on 2/7/07	Price on 2/14/07	Profit/ Loss on 2/14/07	AM Settle Price 2/16/07
Underlying Security	RUT	$783	$816.2	$818.07		$815.99
Buy to Open Put	RUTNB FEB 710	$1				$0
Sell to Open Put	RUTNF FEB 730	$2.14				$0
Sell to Open Call	RUZBF FEB 830	$0.48		$0.20	$0.28	$0
Buy to Open Call	RUZBJ FEB 850	$0.22		$0.05	$(0.17)	$0
Stop Loss for Put		$741	$741	$741		$741
Stop Loss for Call		$818	$820	$822		$822
Net Credit		$1.40			$1.25	$1.40
Profit/Loss if Exit					6.7%	
Maximum Potential Return		7.5%				7.5%

The initial position had a maximum potential return of 7.5 percent. The initial stop-losses were set for 1.5 percent of the option's short strike price; i.e., whenever the RUT index was within 1.5 percent of a short strike price, the offending spread position would be closed. If the RUT were to experience a price of less than $741, then the bull-put credit spread position would be closed, and if the RUT were to transition greater than $818, then the bear-call credit spread position would be closed.

On February 7, 2007, the RUT index experienced a high value of $816.20 for the day, which was close to the upper stop-loss value of $818. Since the position was fairly close to the option's expiration of February 16, 2007, the upper stop-loss was modified from $818 to $820 on February 7, 2007. The new upper stop-loss represents a 1.2 percent stop-loss margin for closing the position.

On February 14, 2007, the RUT index experienced a high value of $817.07 for the day, which was lower than the modified stop-loss of $820. As a result, the position did not experience a stop-loss thanks to the modification. If the stop-loss had not been modified, the position would have been stopped on February 14, 2007 and a profit of 6.7 percent would have been experienced instead of the initial expected profit of 7.5 percent. On February 14, 2007, the upper stop-loss was once again modified from $820 to $822. The new stop-loss represented a 1 percent stop-loss margin.

By moving the stop-loss values, the position did not experience a stop-loss and the RUT index settled AM for $815.99 at expiration on February 16, 2007. Since all options were out-of-the-money, they expired worthless and the initial net credit of $1.40 was kept for a profit of 7.5 percent.

By modifying a stop-loss for the iron condor position, the original maximum potential return of 7.5 percent was experienced instead of the lower return of 6.7 percent, which would have been the case had the position experienced a stop-loss on February 14, 2007 at $818. By modifying the stop-loss slightly, the position was able to experience its full profit potential with only a slight modification in the risk profile.

ROLLING

Rolling is a process for modifying an iron condor position. Rolling typically involves exchanging one position for a similar position with some slight modifications. For example, positions can be rolled to a new month, a new strike price, or a new month and a new strike price. Rolling can be implemented for increasing potential return, extracting profit, or managing risk.

For the iron condor, positions can be rolled in order to increase potential return. Rolling involves replacing a profitable spread position, which has for the most part reached its maximum profit-

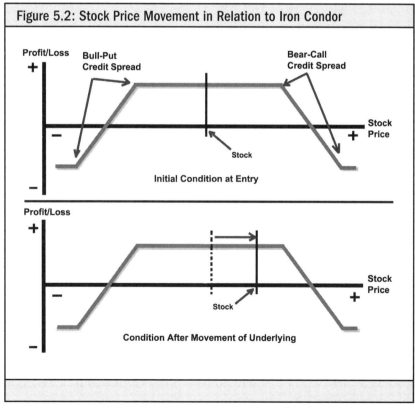

Figure 5.2: Stock Price Movement in Relation to Iron Condor

Source: PowerOptions (www.poweropt.com)

making potential for a new spread position. This has the potential to add additional profit. Iron condors are very conducive for increasing potential return via rolling, as the underlying almost always moves higher or lower after initial entry, as illustrated in Figure 5.2.

The options, which the underlying equity distances itself from, will fall in value, and the spread will become more profitable as the underlying moves further away from the option spread and as time value erosion occurs. If the price of the underlying increases, the options for the bull-put credit spread will decrease in value, which will increase the bull-put spread's profitability. Conversely, if the price of the underlying decreases, the options for the bear-call credit spread will decrease in value and thereby increase the bear-call spread's profitability.

The decrease in the value of options as a result of the movement of the underlying equity presents an opportunity to roll the iron condor position and potentially generate additional income. If the price of the underlying increases after entering the iron condor, then the bull-put credit spread is a candidate to be rolled, as illustrated in Figure 5.3.

Alternatively, if the underlying decreases in price, then the bear-call credit spread can potentially be rolled, as illustrated in Figure 5.4.

When rolling an iron condor, only one spread (two option positions) is modified, with the other spread left unchanged. Typically, the spread, which is not modified, has not experienced a decrease in the values of the options and as a result, a profit has not been realized and it is not a candidate to be rolled. If the underlying equity retraces after executing the initial roll, then it might be possible to roll the spread that was left untouched during the initial roll. There could also be a rare occasion where both of the spreads could be rolled at

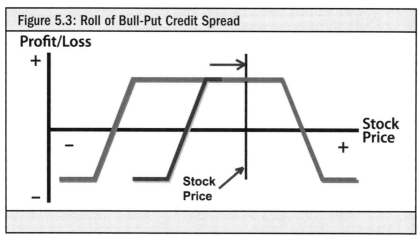

Figure 5.3: Roll of Bull-Put Credit Spread

Source: PowerOptions (www.poweropt.com)

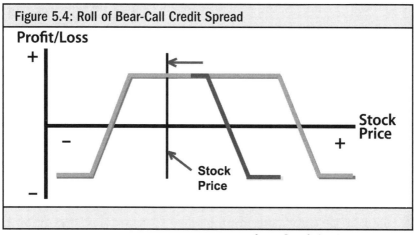

Figure 5.4: Roll of Bear-Call Credit Spread

Source: PowerOptions (www.poweropt.com)

the same time, but brokers do not currently support the capability to enter an eight-leg spread trade, so each spread will have to be rolled via a broker's four-leg spread entry capability.

In order to maintain special margin consideration, rolling an option spread must be performed for the same expiration month and identical separation between the options. For example, if the iron condor's options were initially entered for May expiration, then the new options, which are rolled too, must also be for the month of May. Additionally, if the separation between the short and long option was 10 at entry, then the new rolled differential between the short and long option must also be 10. Rolling the option spreads to a different month or different option separation typically will require additional capital for an iron condor position.

Roll Three or Four

Iron condor positions can be rolled via three-leg or four-leg methods. A four-leg method is the general case for rolling, in which a short option and its corresponding long option are rolled or exchanged for a new short and a new long option. In some cases, the value of the long option does not have significant value and is left open instead of being rolled. For this special case, only three option transactions are required: buy-to-close short option, sell-to-open short option, and buy-to-open long option. Typically, a long option with a value in the range of $0.05 can be left open instead of being rolled.

When to Roll

A rule of thumb for determining when to roll a spread position is based on the ability to capture 80 percent of the maximum potential profit for the spread. A spread position is a candidate to be rolled when 80 percent of the maximum potential profit for either the bull-put or bear-call spread can be captured.

Another consideration for rolling a spread position is the current security or market sentiment. When considering the sentiment of the security or market, a contrarian's attitude should be adopted. For example, if it is desired to roll a bull-put position, then the most opportune time to roll the position is when the current day's price of the market or security is negative. Conversely, the best time to roll a bear-call position is when current day's price is positive, as illustrated in Table 5.8.

Table 5.8: Preferred Sentiment for Rolling Iron Condor

Position to Roll	Preferred Sentiment for Current Day (Contrarian)
Bull-Put	Negative
Bear-Call	Positive

Rolling a bull-put on a day with significant positive sentiment or rolling a bear-call on a day with significant negative sentiment is highly discouraged, as the security or market could have a significant retrace on a following day, potentially causing a loss on the position.

Another strategy for rolling is to close the bull-put spread on a day when the underlying equity is positive, and close the bear-call spread on a day when the underlying is negative. Then on a subsequent day when the market is moving counter to when the spread was closed, the new spread position can be entered. This method has the potential to slightly increase profits, at the expense of increased transaction costs.

It is recommended to not roll a position during the week of expiration, as it is difficult to achieve an attractive risk–reward ratio during this time period.

Entry and Execution for Rolling a Trade

Rolling the bull-put or bear-call portion of an iron condor is fairly straightforward. It's most economical to enter the trade for rolling as a four-leg spread trade with a Limit/Credit amount. Rolling a position by closing the spread position and later opening a new spread position requires significantly more brokerage commissions than rolling via a single four-leg spread order. Additionally, it is easier to get the optimal amount for the roll by using a four-leg spread order with a Limit/Credit, because an order with a Limit/Credit can take advantage of the spreads between the bid and ask prices for all of the options.

For rolling via four legs, the open short option is entered as "buy to close," the open long option is entered as "sell to close," the new short option is designated as "sell to open" and the new long option is designated as "buy to open."

The Limit/Credit can be calculated using the midway point between the bid–ask for each option and then modified as necessary in order to achieve execution of the trade.

For example, suppose we roll the bull-put portion of the previously mentioned iron condor to a new bull-spread position with long put option of OEWQK (May 355) and short put option of OEWQM (May 365). Existing long put option OEWQG (May 335) would be entered as "sell to close," and existing short put option OEWQI (May 345) would be entered as "buy to close." The new long put option OEWQK

(May 355) would be entered as "buy to open" and the new short put option OEWQM (May 365) would be entered as "sell to open." Additionally, the position would be entered as a day order with a net limit credit of $1.00.

An example of a four-leg spread trade entry page for entering the order is shown in Figure 5.5.

If the trade does not execute after a certain time period, an hour for example, we could reduce the net credit limit for the order to $0.95 or $0.90 for the trade to be executed. Reducing the net credit limit could be repeated until the order executes. In general, it is not recommended to roll a position if the additional potential return from rolling is less than 2 percent.

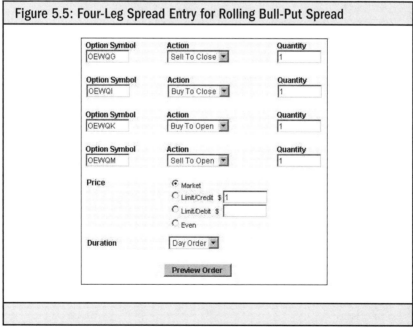

Figure 5.5: Four-Leg Spread Entry for Rolling Bull-Put Spread

Source: PowerOptions (www.poweropt.com)

Rolling Example

To illustrate rolling an iron condor, an example position entered by the PowerOptionsApplied newsletter will be examined.

The initial iron condor position was entered for the NDX index on April 21, 2009. As shown in Table 5.9, the position was selected with a maximum potential return range of 3.5 percent to 4.8 percent based on the bid/ask prices of the stock options.

Table 5.9: Example Rolling Iron Condor

		Open Price 4/21/2009		Roll Price 5/4/2009	
		Bid/Ask	Fill	Bid/Ask	Fill
Underlying Security	NDX	$1,323		$1,428	
Buy to Open Put	NDUQT MAY 1000	$1.15 / 1.40	$1.34		
Sell to Open Put	NDUQA MAY 1025	$1.55 / 1.95	$1.72		
Sell to Open Call	NDVEK MAY 1550	$0.95 / 1.45	$1.12		
Buy to Open Call	NDVEB MAY 1575	$0.50 / 0.85	$0.70		
Sell to Close Put	NDUQT MAY 1000			$0.20 / 0.30	$0.24
Buy to Close Put	NDUQA MAY 1025			$0.25 / 0.45	$0.30
Buy to Open Put	NDUQE MAY 1225			$1.95 / 2.05	$2.05
Sell to Open Put	NDUQO MAY 1250			$2.50 / 3.00	$2.76
Stop-Loss for Put	$1,046			$1,275	
Stop-Loss for Call	$1,519			$1,519	
Net Credit Range		$0.85 / 1.15		$0.50 / 0.80	
Maximum Potential Return Range		3.5% / 4.8%		2.0% / 3.3%	
Initial Net Credit		$1.00		$0.65	
Net Credit Received			$0.80		$0.65
Maximum Potential Return		4.2%	3.3%	2.7%	2.7%
Maximum Potential Return Including Roll				6%	6%

The net credit calculated using the midway point between the bid and the ask price was $1.00, representing a maximum potential return of 4.2 percent. The position was entered with a broker as a contingent day order with lower and upper stop orders of 1,046 and 1,519, respectively, and with a net Credit/Limit of $1.00. Since the volatility of the market was very high, the stop-losses were set for 2 percent of the short option strike prices.

By 3:30 p.m. of the same day (30 minutes left until market close) the position had not executed. The net Credit/Limit for the order was modified from $1.00 to $0.80 and the order was successfully executed with the $0.80 net credit. The net credit of $0.80 represented a maximum potential return of 3.3 percent.

On May 4, 2009, the price of NDX had increased in price from $1,323 to $1,428, about an 8 percent rise in price. The bull-put credit spread portion of the iron condor was profitable and could have been closed for a profit of 1.1 percent. The call options for the bear-call credit spread portion of the iron condor were at approximately the same price as when the position was entered on April 21, 2009 and could have been closed without experiencing a profit or a loss. So on May 4, 2009, the iron condor position could have been closed with a profit of 1.1 percent.

Since the price of the underlying security had moved away from the iron condor's bull-put spread, it was determined to roll the bull-put spread. A new bull-put spread was selected that had a maximum potential return range of 2 to 3.3 percent. This return range included the debit cost of closing the initial bull-put credit spread. The net credit for the order to roll the bull-put was calculated using the midway point between the bid and the ask method. The net credit for rolling was calculated to be $0.65 and was calculated as:

$$= \{\text{bid/ask midway sell put to open} - \text{bid/ask midway buy put to open}\}$$
$$- \{\text{bid/ask midway buy put to close} - \text{bid/ask midway sell put to close}\}$$

$$= \{[\$2.50+(\$3.00-\$2.50)/2] - [\$1.95+(\$2.05-\$1.95)/2]\}$$
$$-\{[\$0.25+(\$0.45-\$0.25)/2] - [\$0.20+(\$0.30-\$0.20)/2]\}$$

$$= \{[\$2.50+(\$0.50)/2] - [\$1.95+(\$0.10)/2]\}$$
$$-\{[\$0.25+(\$0.20)/2] - [\$0.20+(\$0.10)/2]\}$$

$$= \{[\$2.50+\$0.25] - [\$1.95+\$0.05]\}$$
$$-\{[\$0.25+\$0.10] - [\$0.20+\$0.05]\}$$

$$= \{[\$2.75] - [\$2.00]\}$$
$$-\{[\$0.35] - [\$0.25]\}$$

$$= \{\$0.75\} - \{\$0.10\}$$
$$= \$0.65$$

The $0.65 net credit represented an additional potential return of 2.7 percent, which was in addition to the initial potential return of 3.3 percent. The additional potential return resulted in a maximum potential return of 6 percent after the position was rolled.

The roll order was entered as a four-leg spread option with a Net Credit/Limit of $0.65. The order was executed for $0.65 and the original contingent stop order for the bull-put spread was modified from $1,046 to $1,275. The new stop-loss was entered for 2 percent of the short strike price of the new put option.

At market open of expiration day on April 15, 2009, the NDX index AM settled at a price of $1,353.16, which was greater than the rolled put option short strike price of $1,250 and was less than the initial call option short strike price of $1,575. As a result, all of the options expired worthless and the cumulative net credit generated a profit of $1.45 (original net credit of $0.80 + rolled net credit of $0.65) per share of the underlying for a return of 6 percent.

By rolling the iron condor position, the return experienced was almost double the return of the initial position.

IRON CONDOR PORTFOLIO AND ROLLING

When rolling iron condor positions within a portfolio of iron condors, several options are available. The positions can be rolled on different days in order to provide diversity to the positions in the portfolio. Additionally, the positions can be diversified based on whether the bull-put or bear-call spread is rolled.

In some cases, the prices of the underlying of a portfolio of iron condors are near the prices at entry, and the bull-put or the bear-call spreads, or both, can be successfully rolled. In this case, an investor might hedge the portfolio by rolling the bull-put spread for a portion of the iron condor positions and rolling the bear-call spread for the remaining positions. Additionally, an investor might consider rolling both the bull-put and the bear-call spreads for a portion of the iron condor positions.

Diversifying the manner in which the positions are rolled reduces the size of a loss should the market make a dramatic move after the positions have been rolled. For example, if the bull-put spreads are rolled for half of the portfolio positions and the bear-call spreads are rolled for the remainder of positions, and if the market were to move significantly after performing the rolls, then only half of the positions would have a high probability of sustaining a loss. If the market were to fall significantly, then the bull-put spreads, which were rolled, would be in danger of sustaining a loss; and if the market were to rise significantly, then the rolled bear-call spreads would be likely candidates for experiencing a loss. With this scenario, either way the market moves, only half of the positions would be likely to sustain a loss.

As an example, three iron condor positions which were recommended by PowerOptionsApplied's *Chromium* newsletter will be analyzed. The initial position taken for each index is illustrated in Table 5.10.

Table 5.10: Initial Iron Condor Positions for PowerOptionsApplied's Chromium

Index	Date of Entry	Price of Index at Entry	Buy to Open Put	Sell to Open Put	Sell to Open Call	Buy to Open Call	Stop Loss Low	Stop Loss High	Net Credit	Max Pot. Return
NDX	6/22/09	1435	NDUSM JUL 1150	NDUSZ JUL 1175	NDVGM JUL 1650	NDVGD JUL 1675	1199	1617	0.75	3.1%
RUT	6/24/09	500	RURSR JUL 390	RUWSE JUL 410	RUWGN JUL 570	RUWGR JUL 590	418	559	0.60	3.1%
SPX	6/25/09	908	SPZSO JUL 775	SPZSQ JUL 785	SPQGB JUL 1010	SPQGD JUL 1020	801	990	0.35	3.6%

On July 6, 2009, it was determined that the positions should be rolled, but the prices of the indexes were very close to the prices at entry as shown in Table 5.11.

Table 5.11 Comparison of Index Prices at Entry versus July 6, 2009

Index	Price of Index at Entry	Price of Index on July 6, 2009
NDX	1,435	1,441
RUT	500	494
SPX	908	899

The prices of the indexes on July 6, 2009 had only changed about 1 percent or less from entry. And there was no clear indication as to whether the market would move up or down, so the decision was made to split between rolling the bull-put spreads and the bear-call spreads. The bull-put spreads for the NDX and RUT iron condors were rolled up and the bear-call spreads for the SPX iron condor were rolled down, as illustrated in Tables 5.12 and 5.13.

This way, if the market moved down, the NDX and the RUT positions were more likely to encounter a stop-loss, leaving a successful SPX position. If the market moved up, the SPX position would be more likely to sustain a stop-loss, leaving the NDX and RUT positions successful. The decision as to which ones should have their bull-put spreads versus bear-call spreads was determined based on the erosion of the time value of the short call options.

Table 5.12: Rolling Bull-Put Spreads for PowerOptionsApplied's Chromium

Index	Date of Roll	Price of Index at Roll	Sell to Close Put	Buy to Close Put	Sell to Open Put	Buy to Open Put	New Stop Loss Low	Add. Net Credit	Total Net Credit	Max Pot. Return
NDX	7/6/09	1435	NDUSM JUL 1150	NDUSZ JUL 1175	NDUSF JUL 1275	NDUSO JUL 1250	1301	0.40	1.15	4.7%
RUT	7/9/09	479	RURSR JUL 390	RUWSE JUL 410	RUWSO JUL 440	RUWSG JUL 420	449	0.40	1.00	5.2%

Table 5.13: Rolling Bear-Call Spreads for PowerOptionsApplied's Chromium

Index	Date of Roll	Price of Index at Roll	Sell to Close Call	Buy to Close Call	Sell to Open Call	Buy to Open Call	New Stop Loss Hi	Add. Net Credit	Total Net Credit	Max Pot. Return
SPX	7/7/09	881	SPQGD JUL 1020	SPQGB JUL 1010	SXBGK JUL 955	SXBGM JUL 965	941	0.25	0.60	6.2%

The time value for the short put options for the NDX and the RUT had decayed more than the short put options for the SPX, and the time value for the short call options for the SPX had eroded more than for the NDX and the RUT.

In order to diversify, the positions were rolled on different days. Since the put options for the NDX had decayed the most of the three positions, it was the first one rolled, on July 6, 2009. After the NDX, the short call options for the SPX had experienced the largest decay and the SPX was rolled on July 7, 2009. Following the roll of the NDX and the SPX, the RUT was rolled on July 9, 2009.

By rolling the iron condor positions, the aggregate maximum potential return was significantly increased from 3.3 percent to 5.4 percent, yet the probability of success after rolling was comparable to the probability of success at initial entry.

After rolling the positions, the market turned bullish and the SPX position was in danger of experiencing a stop-loss on July 16, 2009, which was the day prior to expiration. Early in the day, we decided not to modify the upper stop-loss since the options for the SPX index are AM settled and Google was scheduled to report earnings after the market closed. If Google announced good earnings numbers, the market could easily have rallied on Friday and the SPX could easily have moved past the 955 short strike price of the rolled short call option, which would mean a significant loss.

For most of the day, the SPX did not experience a stop-loss, and later in the day the upper stop-loss was modified from 941 to 945, which prevented the position from hitting a stop-loss. The SPX did cross the pre-modified stop-loss of 941 prior to the market closing, but did not cross the revised stop-loss value of 945.

When the stop-loss was modified, our belief was that the market would retrace; however, the market started to rally near the market close and it was feared a good earnings report for Google would cause a market rally on Friday. Armed with this information, we decided to close the bear-call spread for the SPX position just before market close on Thursday.

Closing the SPX position early resulted in a -3.5 percent loss on the trade; however, the two other remaining positions were fully profitable and, as a result, the aggregate return for the three iron condors was profitable with a return of 2.1 percent.

After market close on Thursday, Google announced poor earnings and the market did not rally on Friday as was feared. The SPX position did not need to be closed early, but it was better to take a small loss on one position and a smaller profit overall, than take a large loss on one position and a large loss overall.

DIVERSITY OF IRON CONDOR POSITIONS

In general, it is recommended to enter a diverse number of iron condor positions. Diversification spreads out the risk of experiencing simultaneous losses across all positions and aids in experiencing a moderate loss instead of a dramatic loss across an entire portfolio. With diversity it is possible to experience a loss for one iron condor, but experience a profit for the remaining iron condor positions, which allows for a smaller impact overall. Diversifying iron condor positions will not prevent losses from occurring, because any significantly large market movement can cause a disruption even for the most diversified of portfolios.

Iron condor positions for indexes do not have to be significantly diverse; a modicum amount is generally sufficient. For example, even though the S&P 100 and Russell indexes are highly correlated or generally have similar movements, they are uncorrelated or dissimilar enough to aid in preventing simultaneous losses from occurring.

Simply because an index is composed of a multitude of companies does not mean it is significantly diversified. For example, some sector indexes are composed of companies that are very similar and have similar stock movements. A sector index composed of very similar companies can cause problems for iron condors in a similar manner, as illustrated previously with individual stocks. An investor planning to invest in a sector index should look carefully at the companies composing the index to verify the component companies are sufficiently diversified for the iron condor strategy.

Time diversity of iron condor positions can be generated by entering positions on different days. Selecting iron condors on different days allows for overlapping or layering the profitability regions of the iron condors to cover a wider range of price movements, which lessens the chance of experiencing a loss on every position, as illustrated in Figure 5.6.

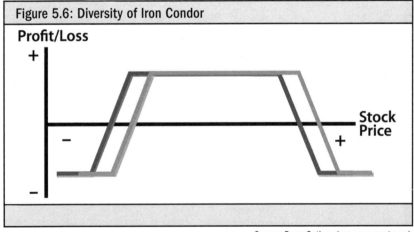

Figure 5.6: Diversity of Iron Condor

Source: PowerOptions (www.poweropt.com)

Diversifying iron condor positions as illustrated in Figure 5.6 reduces the probability of experiencing a loss on every position and also enables the losses experienced in aggregate to be less severe. The downside to the strategy is a requirement for additional management effort and increased brokerage commissions.

SAME MONTH, SAME STRIKE, DIFFERENT ACCOUNTS

A method for diversifying iron condor positions is to enter diverse positions for the same underlying security; however, investors seeking to follow this strategy should be aware that they will not be allowed to have a short and long option with the same expiration month and same strike price in the same trading account. For example, suppose an investor entered an iron condor with a bull-put position for May expiration with a short strike price of $345 as in our previous example. The investor would not be allowed to later enter a bull-put position with May expiration and a long put option with a strike price of $345. An illustration of this concept is shown in Figure 5.7.

MAJOR MARKET EVENT—GET OUT!

Iron condors are best traded in neutral markets. Iron condors also perform well in markets with modest trends; however, iron condors can incur significant losses in markets transitioning from low volatility to high volatility and large or wild price swings.

In general, it is best to exit or partially exit iron condor positions if a market-moving event occurs. Additionally, it is wise to avoid entering new iron condor positions for at least a month after experiencing a market-moving event. Examples of past market–moving events where a premature exit would have been prudent are: 9/11, Hurricane Katrina, and the meltdown of Lehman Brothers.

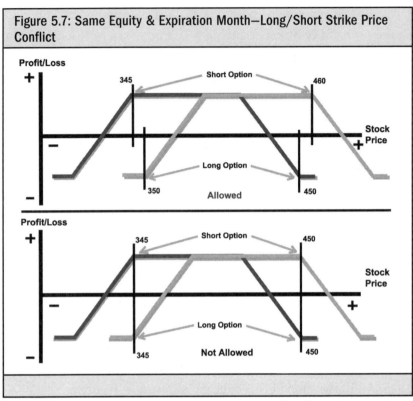

Figure 5.7: Same Equity & Expiration Month—Long/Short Strike Price Conflict

In the event of a market-moving event, an investor can totally exit all iron condor positions or only partially exit the iron condor positions. If the potential market-moving event has a negative bias, then the bull-put portion of the iron condor should be exited, leaving the bear-call portion intact. Conversely, if the potential market-moving event has a positive bias, then the bear-call portion of the iron condor should be exited, leaving the bull-put portion intact.

Generally, potential market-moving events having a negative or bearish bias should be more carefully considered than potential market events with a positive or bullish bias. Market-moving events with a negative bias tend to move the market faster and farther than market–moving events with a positive bias.

In most cases, premature exit of an iron condor will result in a loss on the position; however, the loss resulting from premature exit will be much smaller than exiting later as a result of a stop-loss condition.

After the partial exit of an iron condor due to a potential market-moving event, investors can roll the remaining positions in order to recoup a loss or increase the return of the position. Investors rolling a position in this situation should be very careful not to roll the position too far, as a market reversal can occur, resulting in a loss for the remaining spread position.

TRADE MANAGEMENT TOOLS

Regardless of the stock option strategy implemented, it is important to implement tools for effective management of positions. Generally, brokers provide some tools for management of positions, but these tools are often rudimentary and considered secondary to the tools the brokers provide for the execution of trades.

Monitoring of stock option positions is important and tools for supervising positions should include the ability to provide alerts when certain conditions are met or transgressed. Examples of important alerts are: stock price, option price bid–ask, stock percent change, option percent change, standard moving average, Bollinger Band, and 52–week low and high.

The two most important parameters necessary for monitoring iron condor positions are the underlying price and option percent change.

Alerts for the underlying price are useful for implementing iron condor stop-losses. Alerts for each iron condor position should be monitored for the put and call stop-losses. In the event of a stop-loss, the monitoring tool would provide an alert indicating the position needs some attention. If a contingent order were configured for the position, the trader would use alert information to verify that the broker executed the contingent order. If a contingent was not configured, the trader would perform the necessary steps to manage the stop-loss, i.e., close option positions.

Alerts for option percent change are useful for rolling iron condor positions. A general rule of thumb is to consider rolling an iron condor position when the value of a short option has decreased by more than 80 percent.

An example of a tool alerting traders of conditions for rolling iron condors using PowerOptions is shown in Figure 5.8.

As can be seen, the value of short put option RURRR has decreased by 95.2 percent and is a candidate for rolling, as its value has decreased more than 80 percent. The PowerOptions tool provides an alert indication that the iron condor is in a position to be considered for rolling. Additionally, alerts for the put and call stop-loss have been set for $398 and $588, respectively. The value for RUT is at $508.61, so neither of the stop-losses has been transgressed and the position does not require steps for resolving a stop-loss. Figure 5.9 on page 160 illustrates a subset of the various alerts that can be set using PowerOptions tools.

Figure 5.10 on page 161 illustrates the use of PowerOptions BrokerLink interface for closing short put option RURRR in the event that a stop-loss is encountered.

Figure 5.8: Alert for Rolling Iron Condor

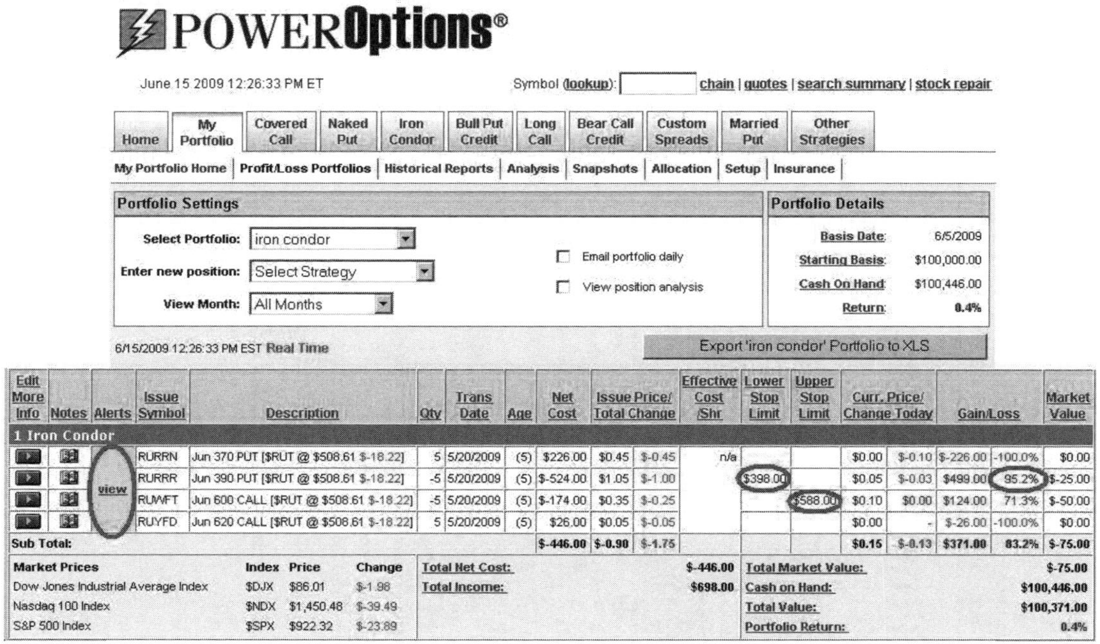

Source: PowerOptions (www.poweropt.com)

Figure 5.9: Setting Alerts for PowerOptions

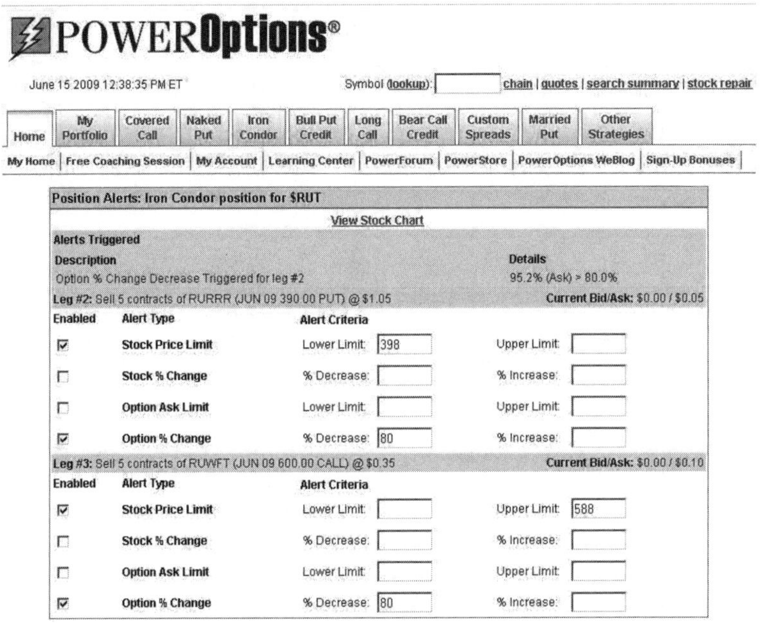

⚡POWER Options®

June 15 2009 12:38:35 PM ET   Symbol (lookup): [   ]   chain | quotes | search summary | stock repair

Home	My Portfolio	Covered Call	Naked Put	Iron Condor	Bull Put Credit	Long Call	Bear Call Credit	Custom Spreads	Married Put	Other Strategies

My Home | Free Coaching Session | My Account | Learning Center | PowerForum | PowerStore | PowerOptions WeBlog | Sign-Up Bonuses

Position Alerts: Iron Condor position for $RUT

View Stock Chart

Alerts Triggered

Description	Details
Option % Change Decrease Triggered for leg #2	95.2% (Ask) > 80.0%

Leg #2: Sell 5 contracts of RURRR (JUN 09 390.00 PUT) @ $1.05   **Current Bid/Ask:** $0.00 / $0.05

Enabled	Alert Type	Alert Criteria			
☑	Stock Price Limit	Lower Limit:	398	Upper Limit:	
☐	Stock % Change	% Decrease:		% Increase:	
☐	Option Ask Limit	Lower Limit:		Upper Limit:	
☑	Option % Change	% Decrease:	80	% Increase:	

Leg #3: Sell 5 contracts of RUWFT (JUN 09 600.00 CALL) @ $0.35   **Current Bid/Ask:** $0.00 / $0.10

Enabled	Alert Type	Alert Criteria			
☑	Stock Price Limit	Lower Limit:		Upper Limit:	588
☐	Stock % Change	% Decrease:		% Increase:	
☐	Option Ask Limit	Lower Limit:		Upper Limit:	
☑	Option % Change	% Decrease:	80	% Increase:	

Source: PowerOptions (www.poweropt.com)

Figure 5.10: Closing Short Put Option Using BrokerLink in the Event of Stop-Loss

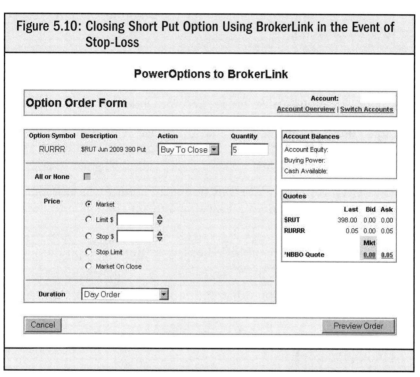

Source: PowerOptions (www.poweropt.com)

IMPORTANT CONCEPTS FROM THIS CHAPTER

- Management strategy for iron condors should be considered prior to entry.

- Predetermined stop-losses are recommended for iron condors.

- Management of iron condors following a stop-loss requires careful consideration.

- Following a stop-loss, long options can be closed, left open, or partially closed and partially left open.

- Contingent stop-loss orders are recommended for iron condors.

- Iron condors with special margin consideration may require additional margin in order for a position to be modified after experiencing a stop-loss.

- Diversifying iron condor positions can reduce the amount of reserve margin required for closing an iron condor in the event of a stop-loss.

- Stop-losses should be modified based on time-to-expiration and current market conditions.

- Iron condors can be rolled in order to potentially generate more return.

- It is best to roll iron condors via a four-leg trade and a Limit/Credit order.

- A portfolio approach can be applied when rolling iron condors.

- Iron condors can be diversified via the underlying equities selected and by time of entry.

- When a major market event occurs, it is best to close or partially close iron condor positions.

- Trade management tools should be considered for monitoring and managing iron condor positions.

REVIEW QUESTIONS FOR CHAPTER 5

1. When experiencing a stop-loss, an investor should immediately:

    A. Close short options closest to the underlying price

    B. Close long options closest to the underlying price

    C. Close long and short options closest to the underlying price

    D. Close all options

    E. None of the above

2. The more diversified a portfolio of iron condors:

    A. The larger the capital reserve required with special margin

    B. The smaller the capital reserve required with special margin

    C. The larger the capital reserve required

    D. The smaller the capital reserve required

    E. None of the above

3. Rolling an iron condor is most efficient and profitable with:

    A. Two-leg market order

    B. Two-leg limit/credit order

    C. Four-leg market order

    D. Four-leg limit/credit order

    E. None of the above

4. The following is not allowed in a brokerage account:

   A. Short call option and long put option with same strike and expiration

   B. Short call option and long call option with same strike and expiration

   C. Short put option and long call option with same strike and expiration

   D. None of the above

5. Immediately following a major market event, iron condor positions should be:

   A. Added to

   B. Exited

   C. None of the above

 Go to the Traders' Library Education Corner at www.traderslibrary.com/TLEcorner for answers to these self-test questions.

Chapter 6

ACTUAL RESULTS

Theory is nice, practice makes perfect, but real world results of the iron condor strategy can give some practical insight into its true power.

PowerOptionsApplied, an advisory newsletter service, has been trading and tracking iron condor trades for indexes for several years. The results for two of the iron condor advisory services from December of 2005 to December of 2009 are shown in Table 6.1.

Table 6.1: Actual Cumulative Returns for Iron Condors, December 2005 to December 2009

Advisory Newsletter	Maximum Expected Return	Success Rate	1 Year (12 months) (%)	2 Year (24 months) (%)	3 Year (36 months) (%)	4 Year (48 months) (%)
Meridian	2-4%	85%	41%	13%	29%	43%
Optium	6-8%	79%	81%	45%	53%	107%

Based on Table 6.1, the returns for the iron condor strategy over the most recent year were phenomenal with returns of 41 percent and 81 percent for Meridian and Optium, respectively. The most recent year's returns are extraordinary, as Meridian and Optium lost -28 percent and -36 percent, respectively two years ago. But these losses are not too bad when considering that the overall stock market took a free-fall of around -50 percent over the same time period! An Optium investor experiencing a one-year negative return of -36 percent might feel pretty good about being in the black instead of the red after recovering the following year with an 81 percent return while the stock market over the same two-year time period was still down about -25 percent.

By just following the advice suggested in this book for exiting and avoiding iron condor positions for one month following a major market event, the actual returns for the two advisory newsletter services would have been greatly improved. For example, simply exiting current iron condor positions and avoiding new iron condor positions following the meltdown of Lehman Brothers would have resulted in yearly returns as shown in Table 6.2.

Table 6.2: Iron Condor Cumulative Returns by Exiting and Waiting One Month after Lehman Brothers Failure, December 2005 to December 2009

Advisory Newsletter	Maximum Expected Return	1 Year (12 months) (%)	2 Year (24 months) (%)	3 Year (36 months) (%)	4 Year (48 months) (%)
Meridian	2-4%	41%	48%	64%	78%
Optium	6-8%	81%	73%	81%	135%

The results of Table 6.2 are much improved; however, to experience these returns, iron condor traders must be able to recognize the occurrence of major market moving events and react appropriately.

REVIEW QUESTIONS FOR CHAPTER 6

1. The authors of this book:

   A. Follow their own advice

   B. Should follow their own advice

   C. None of the above

2. Iron condor traders must be able to recognize and react appropriately:

   A. When playing golf and hearing someone yell "Fore!"

   B. When facing a head-on collision with an eighteen-wheeler

   C. When a major market-moving event occurs

   D. When running with the bulls in Pamplona

 Go to the Traders' Library Education Corner at www.traderslibrary.com/TLEcorner for answers to these self-test questions.

Chapter 7

IRON CONDOR VARIATIONS

IRON BUTTERFLY

The "iron butterfly" position is a special case of an iron condor where the short put options and the short call options have identical strike prices. A profit and loss diagram for the iron butterfly strategy is shown in Figure 7.1.

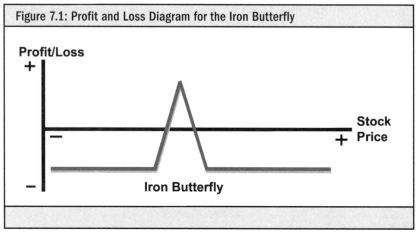

Figure 7.1: Profit and Loss Diagram for the Iron Butterfly

Source: PowerOptions (www.poweropt.com)

As you can see in Figure 7.1, the iron butterfly has a very narrow profitability region as compared to an iron condor; however, the maximum potential profit for an iron butterfly is greater than for an iron condor, all else being equal.

An iron butterfly is best applied to securities that are stuck in a trading range and unlikely to venture from the trading range prior to expiration.

An example search for an iron butterfly on April 13, 2009 using PowerOptions tools is shown in Figure 7.2.

In previous iron condor, bull-put, and bear-call examples, the positions were selected on April 13, 2009 with the OEX index as the underlying. The search results shown in Figure 7.2 were similarly found on April 13, 2009 for the OEX index.

The returns for the iron condor, bull-put, and bear-call examples illustrated previously all had potential returns of less than 20 percent and "probabilities between" of greater than 80 percent. As can be seen in Figure 7.2, iron butterfly positions for OEX on April 13, 2009

Figure 7.2: Iron Butterfly Search Using PowerOptions

More Info	Stock Sym	Company Name	Last Stock Price & Chg	Exp Date	Buy Put Ask	Buy Put Strike	Sell Put Bid	Sell Put Strike	Sell Call Bid	Sell Call Strike	Buy Call Ask	Buy Call Strike	Lower Break Even	Upper Break Even	Total Net Credit	% Return	% Prob Between	Max Risk
	$OEX	S&P 100 Index	402.95 (+0.88)	MAY 16 2009	7.40	375.0	15.40	400.0	17.20	400.0	7.10	425.0	381.90	418.10	18.10	262.3	33.5	6.81
	$OEX	S&P 100 Index	402.95 (+0.88)	MAY 16 2009	9.60	380.0	17.80	405.0	14.60	405.0	6.05	430.0	387.10	422.90	17.90	252.1	33.5	7.10
	$OEX	S&P 100 Index	402.95 (+0.88)	MAY 16 2009	10.30	385.0	20.50	410.0	12.10	410.0	4.60	435.0	392.30	427.70	17.70	242.5	33.3	7.30
	$OEX	S&P 100 Index	402.95 (+0.88)	MAY 16 2009	6.30	370.0	13.30	395.0	20.10	395.0	6.90	420.0	376.80	413.20	18.20	267.6	33.0	6.80
	$OEX	S&P 100 Index	402.95 (+0.88)	MAY 16 2009	12.00	390.0	23.20	415.0	10.10	415.0	3.70	440.0	397.40	432.60	17.60	237.8	32.0	7.40
	$OEX	S&P 100 Index	402.95 (+0.88)	MAY 16 2009	5.30	365.0	11.30	390.0	23.20	390.0	10.80	415.0	371.60	408.40	18.40	278.8	31.6	6.60
	$OEX	S&P 100 Index	402.95 (+0.88)	MAY 16 2009	14.00	395.0	26.40	420.0	8.20	420.0	2.80	445.0	402.20	437.80	17.80	247.2	31.3	7.20
	$OEX	S&P 100 Index	402.95 (+0.88)	MAY 16 2009	16.20	400.0	28.30	425.0	6.50	425.0	2.15	450.0	408.55	441.45	16.45	192.4	28.4	8.55
	$OEX	S&P 100 Index	402.95 (+0.88)	MAY 16 2009	12.00	390.0	20.50	410.0	12.10	410.0	5.80	430.0	395.20	424.80	14.80	284.6	28.2	5.20

Source: PowerOptions (www.poweropt.com)

have potential returns in excess of 200 percent and "probabilities between" of less than 35 percent. Although the iron butterfly positions have larger potential returns, their likelihood of generating a profit is much less.

The highlighted iron butterfly position in Figure 7.2 is entered by purchasing an OEWQO (MAY 375) put option for $7.40, selling an OXBQT (MAY 400) put option for $15.40, selling an OXBET (MAY 400) call option for $17.20, and purchasing an OXBEE (MAY 425) call option for $7.10. As can be seen, the short put option and the long call option have the same strike price of $400. The total net credit for the position is $18.10. The maximum risk for the position is $6.90, which is calculated as the total net credit subtracted from the margin requirement, or $25-$18.10. The margin requirement for the iron butterfly is the same as for the iron condor illustrated previously in Chapter 2.

The lower break-even point of $381.90 is calculated as total net credit subtracted from the sold put option's strike price, or $400-$18.10. The upper break-even point of $418.10 is calculated as the sum of the total net credit and the short option's strike price, or $400+$18.10. The lower and upper break-even points are the break-even for the position at expiration. The profit and loss diagram for the highlighted iron butterfly position is illustrated in Figure 7.3.

For an expiration price of OEX less than $375 and greater than $425, a loss is experienced for the entire amount of margin at risk, or $690 per contract.

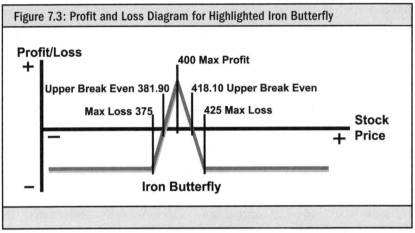

Figure 7.3: Profit and Loss Diagram for Highlighted Iron Butterfly

Source: PowerOptions (www.poweropt.com)

The example OEX iron butterfly has a significantly greater maximum potential return—262 percent—than the previously illustrated OEX iron condor's maximum potential return of 10.5 percent, but it is at the expense of a smaller profitability region and lower probability of success.

DOUBLE DIAGONAL

The "double diagonal" stock options position is a special case of an iron condor where the expiration month for the purchased options is further out in time than the expiration month for the sold options. For example, for short options expiring in May, the long options might expire in the June, July, or August, etc.

The main strength of the double diagonal strategy is its capability to perform in markets with low volatility; markets where a traditional iron condor has a tendency to not perform very well. The long options of the double diagonal with expiration farther out in time than the short options are more sensitive to changes in volatility. An

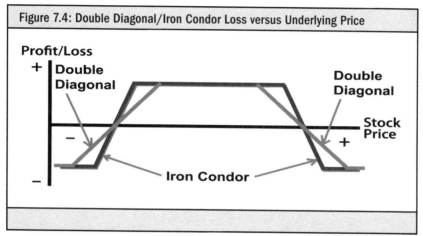

Figure 7.4: Double Diagonal/Iron Condor Loss versus Underlying Price

Source: PowerOptions (www.poweropt.com)

increase in volatility will increase the value of the long options. So, for a market with low volatility in which volatility suddenly spikes, the long options of the double diagonal increase in value relative to the short options; this aids in increasing profitability or ameliorating a loss.

Another strength of the double diagonal strategy is how the wings of the iron condor tend to fall off more slowly with respect to the movement of the underlying, as illustrated in Figure 7.4.

For example, consider the double diagonal position for ETF QQQQ as illustrated in Table 7.1.

Table 7.1: Double Diagonal for ETF QQQQ

Action	Option Symbol	Month/Expiration/Option	Price
BTO	QAVWF	Nov 32 Put	$0.14
STC	QQQVL	Oct 38 Put	$0.32
STC	QQQJR	Oct 44 Call	$0.22
BTO	QQQKU	Nov 47 Call	$0.13

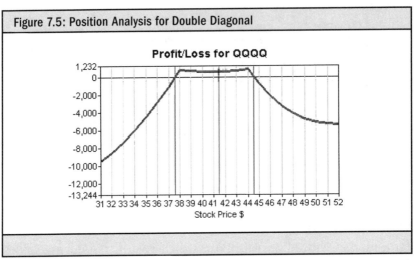

Figure 7.5: Position Analysis for Double Diagonal

Source: PowerOptions (www.poweropt.com)

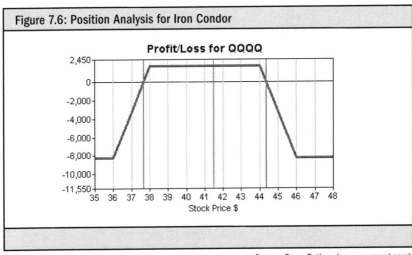

Figure 7.6: Position Analysis for Iron Condor

Source: PowerOptions (www.poweropt.com)

A profit and loss graph for the QQQQ double diagonal position, as illustrated in Table 7.1, generated by the PowerOptions Position Analysis tool, is shown in Figure 7.5.

Let's compare the double diagonal position just illustrated with an iron condor position as shown in Table 7.2. The iron condor position has the same short stock options, but different long stock options. The double diagonal has long options with expiration in November versus the iron condor, which has long options with expiration in October.

Table 7.2: Iron Condor for ETF QQQQ

Action	Option Symbol	Month/Expiration/Option	Price
BTO	QQQVJ	Oct 36 Put	$0.15
STC	QQQVL	Oct 38 Put	$0.32
STC	QQQJR	Oct 44 Call	$0.22
BTO	QQQJT	Oct 46 Call	$0.04

A profit and loss graph for the QQQQ iron condor position, as illustrated in Table 7.2, generated by the PowerOptions Position Analysis tool, is shown in Figure 7.6.

As illustrated in Figures 7.5 and 7.6, the double diagonal has a much slower rate of loss over the iron condor, as the price of the underlying transitions to less than the short put strike price, or as the price of the underlying transitions to greater than the short call strike price.

In general, a stop-loss for a double diagonal will incur a smaller loss than for an iron condor, all else being equal.

Double diagonals have several disadvantages compared to iron condors.

- They are not eligible for special margin;

- They require large amounts of capital for indexes (alternative is ETFs);

- They are not eligible for special tax considerations with ETFs;

- Their profitability region is generally not as wide as an iron condor;

- Their return calculation is not as straightforward as an iron condor; and,

- They require more management than an iron condor.

No Special Margin

A drawback to the double diagonal is that brokers generally do not provide special margin for the position because all of the options do not have the same month of expiration.

Large Capital Requirement for Indexes

Additionally, double diagonals for index positions with wide profitability regions tend to require a significant amount of capital per contract. For example, a double diagonal position for an index might require $25,000 for one contract, which is out of reach for many investors. Or, a double diagonal position may not allow investors to adequately diversify their portfolios.

On the other hand, double diagonal positions with fairly wide profitability regions can typically be entered for ETFs for only a couple thousand dollars. Unfortunately, double diagonals with ETFs as the underlying do not allow investors to take advantage of the special tax considerations available for an iron condor with an index as the underlying.

Smaller Profitability Region

In general, a double diagonal position will not have as wide a profitability region as an iron condor, all else being equal.

Return Calculation Complicated

The maximum potential return calculation for double diagonals is not as straightforward as for iron condors. The return calculation for double diagonals does not assume the value of the long options will be zero at the expiration of the short options, as in the case with iron condors. The long options for the double diagonal are further out in time and will not expire simultaneously with the short options, and will have some quantity of value at the expiration of the short option.

The value for the long options at the short option expiration is commonly calculated via the Black-Scholes option pricing model. The value derived from this model is dependent on the volatility of the stock market, which is subject to change and assumes the stock market behaves in a Gaussian manner. Assuming the market behaves in a Gaussian manner is a source of inaccuracy for options, as discussed in Chapter 2, especially for options significantly out-of-the-money as in the case of the long options for the double diagonal strategy. Based on this, the theoretical potential return calculation for a double diagonal position should be considered approximate and not as firm as for the iron condor.

Require More Management

For profitable positions, double diagonals require more management than iron condors. Profitable iron condor positions typically require no additional management, as the options all expire worthless. Conversely, profitable double diagonals require investors to close or roll the long option positions at some point. Also, since the profitability regions of double diagonals are typically smaller than iron condors, more management of the positions is required for rolling the trades.

REVIEW QUESTIONS FOR CHAPTER 7

1. Advantages of the double diagonal as compared to the iron condor are:

   A. Can perform in low volatile market conditions
   B. Generally incurs a smaller loss after a stop-loss is experienced
   C. All of the above
   D. None of the above

2. Disadvantages of the double diagonal as compared to the iron condor are:

   A. Not eligible for special margin
   B. Profitability region generally not as wide
   C. Requires more management
   D. All of the above
   E. None of the above

3. Trading iron butterflies is best suited for stocks that:

   A. Have wide price swings
   B. Are stuck in a trading range
   C. Are in the Iron Flower industry

4. Compared to iron condors, iron butterflies:

   A. Have more potential return, all else being equal
   B. Have less potential return, all else being equal
   C. Come from iron caterpillars
   D. Are hatched from iron eggs

 Go to the Traders' Library Education Corner at
www.traderslibrary.com/TLEcorner for answers to these self-test questions.

Chapter 8

REVIEW

The purpose of this text was to introduce the iron condor with a bias toward real world practical implementations of the strategy. Investors of all experience levels can benefit from the information provided. Highly technical information related to the strategy has been intentionally excluded in order to avoid confusing and confounding readers. The technical information excluded is peripheral to the successful implementation of an iron condor strategy. The excluded information is analogous to the instrument gauges of an automobile. A driver of an automobile does not require an oil pressure gauge or tachometer to drive the vehicle, but instrument gauges are useful for observing the real-time condition of the automobile. Similarly, the excluded technical information is not necessary for trading iron condors, though it may useful for observing the real-time conditions of a position. This chapter will review points we have learned here.

CHAPTER 1

Chapter 1 introduced options and, in particular, presented a basic high-level overview of the iron condor strategy. The most important points to be gained from Chapter 1 are: iron condor positions should only be implemented in a diversified portfolio, and iron condor positions have the potential to experience very large losses and should not be a large portion of an investor's portfolio. The iron condor is a neutral strategy, which matches well with the overall behavior of the stock market. The behavior of the stock market is generally stagnant, but experiences infrequent, brief periods of very large movements. The iron condor strategy typically works well in markets moving less than 5 percent (up or down) per month.

CHAPTER 2

Chapter 2 introduced the basic theory behind the iron condor strategy. The iron condor is a combination of two popular strategies: the bull-put credit spread and bear-call credit spread. The method for calculating the margin requirements and maximum potential return for the bull-put, bear-call, and iron condor were introduced. Special margin considerations for iron condors have a significant positive impact on maximum potential returns. Some background information related to theoretical probability calculations for iron condors was made available.

Investors must realize the popular Black-Scholes option pricing model experiences some inaccuracies when applied to the iron condor. The Black-Scholes model assumes the stock market behaves with a Gaussian distribution, but in reality, the distribution of the stock market experiences fatter tails and is narrower about the mean than the Gaussian distribution. As a result, the probabilities of success, as presented by the Black-Scholes option pricing model for iron condors, will generally be more optimistic than what is actually experienced in the real market. The histogram method for calculating the probabilities of success for iron condors was briefly mentioned and compared to the Black-Scholes model. While the histogram method for calculating iron condor probabilities presents a more real-world view of the strategy, it requires an increased number of calculations to be performed compared to the Black-Scholes model.

CHAPTER 3

Chapter 3 discussed the various equities available for iron condors and their relative advantages and disadvantages. Applying the iron condor strategy to ETFs and indexes is considered more plausible than implementation with individual stocks. Implementing iron condors for individual stocks is generally discouraged. The relative advantages and disadvantages of ETFs versus indexes were explored.

The main ideas presented relating to iron condor indexes and ETFs are: AM settlement for iron condor indexes must be managed very carefully, and iron condor ETFs are not considered applicable for special Section 1256 tax advantages. It is important to consider the style of the options comprising an iron condor, whether American or European. Iron condors with European style options do not require monitoring for exercise; however, iron condors with American style options must be monitored for susceptibility to exercise, and then be managed accordingly.

CHAPTER 4

Chapter 4 covered the mechanics of finding and trading iron condors. The areas of consideration for selecting a broker for trade execution were discussed. Cost is a main driver for selecting a broker, but not the only issue to be considered. Other issues to be considered for broker selection include: capital and trading level requirements, margin considerations, order execution and efficiency, analysis tools, and technical support. The variables controlling the success of iron condors are discussed: initial expected return, average expected loss, probability of success, stop-losses, time-to-expiration, and bid–ask. The daunting task of finding appropriate iron condor positions with more than two million available choices is discussed, as well as available tools for honing the search. The intricacies of entering an iron condor position are briefly discussed.

CHAPTER 5

Chapter 5 discussed the management of iron condor positions. Initial selection and the subsequent volatility of the market will dictate the level of management required for an iron condor. Positions with higher potential return will require a subsequently higher level of management to be performed. Implementation of stop-losses for iron condors is highly encouraged. Methods for the management of iron condor positions following stop-losses were considered.

Management of stop-losses can have a drastic effect on the returns experienced for iron condors, both positive and negative. Contingent stop-loss orders are encouraged, yet, the only brokers known to currently provide this capability are optionsXpress and optionsMONSTER. Capital requirements for stop-losses were discussed, as well as considerations for modifying stop-losses. Rolling of iron condor positions with the intent of increasing maximum potential returns was explained. Time-diversification of iron condor positions was discussed, as well as potential position conflicts, which are not allowed within a brokerage account. The most important idea presented in this chapter was for iron condors to be exited or partially exited following a major market event. Long-term returns for the iron condor strategy are heavily influenced by the capability to recognize and act following a major market event.

CHAPTER 6

Chapter 6 analyzed real-world iron condor returns for PowerOptionsApplied's newsletters. While not stellar, the returns are decent considering the free-fall the markets experienced in 2008. The newsletter returns would have been spectacular if the advice on exiting iron condor positions as presented in this text had been taken following the bankruptcy of Lehman Brothers.

CHAPTER 7

The iron butterfly and the double diagonal, variations of the iron condor strategy, were considered in Chapter 7. While the double diagonal is advantageous with respect to average losses being less than for the iron condor, it experiences disadvantages with respect to special margin, tax considerations, profitability region, and management.

GLOSSARY

Action – Defines the type of trade the investor is entering. The standard actions when entering a trade are Buy to Open or Sell to Open. When closing a position, the standard actions are Buy to Close or Sell to Close.

Aggressive Investor – An investor that looks to trade positions with a high potential return, little or no protection and a slim probability of earning the potential return.

All or None – A type of trade order that can be placed to assure the investor receives all shares or option contracts of a potential trade at a specific price set by the investor. If all shares or option contracts cannot be filled at the specific price, then no shares or option contracts will be traded.

American-Style Option – This kind of option contract may be exercised or assigned at any time between the date of purchase/write and the expiration date. Most exchange-traded options are American-style.

AM Settlement – Options whose values are based on an index which is settled or determined based on the aggregate market opening price or the price of the first trade of each component of the index on options expiration day.

Ask Price – The price that sellers are trying to get for an equity or option on the open market. The ask price will usually be higher than the last trade price, since most investors are trying to sell at the highest price the market will support. The ask price is the most likely price a buyer will pay for an equity or option when placing a market order.

Assignment – The action an option seller encounters when the option buyer exercises their rights and the option seller has to fulfill their obligations. For a short call, assignment occurs when the call seller has to deliver shares of stock; for a short put, assignment occurs when the put seller is forced to buy shares of stock at the strike price.

At-the-Money (ATM) – An option whose strike price is equal to the price of its underlying stock. When the stock price is very close to the strike price but not equal it is said to be near-the-money. Near-the-Money and At-the-Money options tend to have the most time premium.

Back Testing – The practice of using historical data in order to analyze past performance of a particular trading methodology. The SmartHistoryXL tool mentioned in Chapter 4 is a useful tool for back testing options strategies.

Bear-Call Credit Spread – A neutral-to-bearish strategy entered by selling an at-the-money or out-of-the-money call option, while at the same time purchasing a deeper out-of-the-money call option with the same expiration date.

Bearish Sentiment – The sentiment that a stock or the market in general will decline in price.

Bid Price – The price that buyers are trying to get for an equity or option on the open market. This price will usually be lower than the last trade price since buyers would like to pay the lowest amount possible for an equity or option. The bid price is the most likely price a seller will collect for an equity or option when placing a market order.

Bid-Ask Spread – The price spread between the bid price (what a seller is most likely to receive) and the ask price (what a buyer is most likely to pay) for an equity or an option. Both sellers and buyers will try to maximize their trades by entering a limit order for a value that is between the bid-ask spread.

Black-Scholes Model – The Black-Scholes Model is a theoretical pricing model for options developed by Fischer Black and Myron Scholes. It is based on 5 factors: (1) the underlying stock price; (2) the strike price of the option; (3) days remaining to expiration; (4) current interest rates; and (5) the underlying stock volatility.

Black-Scholes Ratio – By comparing an option's Black-Scholes theoretical value to its current trading price, an investor can assess whether the option might be overvalued or undervalued. The B-S Ratio is calculated by taking the trading price of the option divided by the Black-Scholes theoretical worth for that option. Therefore, a B-S Ratio of 1.2 tells us that the option is overvalued by 20 percent. A B-S Ratio of -0.8 tells us that the option is undervalued by 20 percent.

Break Even – The stock price at which any option strategy or combination stock and option strategy has a zero loss and a zero gain.

% to Break Even – The percentage a stock can change in value before the break even price is hit in any option strategy or combination stock and option strategy.

Bullish Sentiment – The sentiment that a stock or the market in general will rise in price.

Bull-Put Credit Spread – A neutral-to-bullish strategy entered by selling a put option at or out-of-the-money, while at the same time purchasing a deeper out-of-the-money put option with the same expiration date.

Buy and Hold – An investment strategy in which an investor will purchase stock, mutual funds, or ETFs and hope that the underlying security rises in value over time so the investor realizes a profit.

Buy to Close or BTC – A type of investment action where an investor will buy back any option contracts that have been sold in order to cancel the fulfillment requirements or obligations.

Buy to Open or BTO – A type of investment action where an investor will buy into an equity or option contract to speculate on the movement of the underlying security.

Buyer – A purchaser or speculator of an equity or option contract.

Call Option – A contract that offers the owner the right, but not the obligation to purchase stock at the strike price before the expiration date. One option contract gives the right to control 100 shares of the underlying stock until expiration, unless the contract otherwise specifies.

Commissions – The price a broker will charge for an equity or option transaction.

Conservative Investor – An investor who looks to trade positions with a decent potential return, high protection, and a high probability of earning the potential return.

Covered Position – An investment strategy where short call contracts are protected by ownership of an equal number of shares of the underlying security (covered call) or an equal number of purchased call contracts at a different strike (credit or debit spread); or, where short put contracts are protected by an equal number of short stock (covered put) or an equal number of purchased put contracts (credit or debit spread).

Credit Spread – An option investment strategy where an investor receives a credit for selling call or put options while buying an equal or different amount of call or put options on the same underlying security. If an investor sells call options and buys an equal number of call options at a higher strike price and receives a credit, the position is a Bear Call Credit Spread. If an investor sells put options and buys an equal number of put options at a lower strike price, the position is a Bull Put Credit Spread.

Day Order – A duration order that can be placed with a broker such that the order will remain open until fulfillment or until the end of the trading day the order was placed.

Debit Spread – An option investment strategy where an investor pays a debit for selling call or put options while buying an equal or different amount of call or put options on the same underlying security. If an investor sells call options and buys an equal number of call options at a lower strike price and pays a debit, the position is a Bull Call Debit Spread. If an investor sells put options and buys an equal number of put options at a higher strike price, the position is a Bear Put Debit Spread.

Delta – Delta is a measure of the sensitivity the option value has to changes in the underlying equity price. For every dollar of movement in the stock price, the price of the option can be expected to move by delta points. Puts have a negative delta. If the delta is -0.5, then a one point increase in the underlying equity price will cause the put to lose $0.50 in value. A put option that is deep out-of-the-money (OTM) will have a delta close to zero. A put option that is deep in-the-money (ITM) will have a delta close to -1.

European Style Option – Option which can only be exercised on the option's expiration date.

Exchange Traded Fund or ETF – Exchange Traded Funds (ETFs) trade much like stocks and can hold assets like stocks and bonds. ETFs typically trade at the aggregate price of the underlying assets making up the fund. ETFs typically charge an annual fee of in the range of 0.1% to 1%.

European Style – This kind of option contract may be exercised only during a specified period of time just prior to its expiration date.

Exercise – The action an option buyer takes to force the option seller to fulfill their obligations. When a call owner exercises their contract, the call owner will purchase shares of stock from the call seller. When a put owner exercises their contract, the put seller is forced to buy shares of stock.

Expiration Date – The date on which an option and the right to exercise it or have it assigned cease to exist. For most equity options, the expiration date is the third Friday of the designated expiration month.

Expire (Worthless) – The action when an option is out-of-the-money (OTM) at expiration and ceases to exist without any intrinsic value.

Fundamental Criteria – The financial values of a stock that are used to determine the strength or weakness of the company. Some fundamental criteria include earnings, earnings growth, cash flow, and sales.

Future Expiration Value – The expected value of the equity or combination equity and option transaction at the expiration date, assuming the equity remains at the current value through expiration. This value is shown on the PowerOptions Profit/Loss Portfolio and Position Analysis tool for management calculations.

Gamma – The rate at which an option's delta changes as the price of the underlying changes. Gamma is usually expressed in deltas gained or lost per a one point change in the underlying equity. As an example, if gamma is .05 the option's delta would change .05 if the underlying equity moved one point.

Good Till Canceled – A duration order that can be placed with a broker such that the order will remain open until fulfillment or until canceled by the investor.

Greeks – Options criteria that measure how the instrument will change in price due to changes in the underlying equity, volatility of the stock, or interest rates in the market.

Implied Volatility – The stock volatility that is implied by the actual trading price of the option. The Black-Scholes model is used to back calculate what volatility must be to create the present price of the option.

Income Generating Strategy – Stock option investment strategy where a premium or credit is received on a regular basis. These strategies include the iron condor, naked put, covered call, credit spread, and others.

Index – An index value is generally based on the prices of an underlying basket of securities.

Index Options – Option contracts that are available on an index such as the S&P 500 index, the Nasdaq 100 index, or the Russell 2000. Indexes represent a collection of various stocks and typically have a lower historical volatility as they do not fluctuate in price as frequently as individual stocks.

Individual Retirement Account or IRA – Investment account with special tax benefits and consequences. There are several different types of IRAs: Traditional, Roth, etc.

In-the-Money (ITM) – This phrase describes where the underlying stock price falls relative to the option strike price. For put options, it is when the price of the stock is lower than the strike price of the option. For call options, it is when the stock price is above the strike price of the option.

% In-the-Money – This is where the underlying stock price falls relative to the option strike price, expressed as a percentage.

Intrinsic Value – Every option premium is comprised of some intrinsic value and some time value. The intrinsic value is based on how deep in the money the stock is priced. For a put, it is how far below the strike price the stock price is located.

Iron Condor – Neutral stock options strategy consisting of a combination of a Bull-Put Credit Spread and a Bear-Call Credit Spread. An Iron Condor is entered by selling two short options, a put and a call, and purchasing two long options, a put and a call. All of the options for an Iron Condor have the same expiration month.

LEAPs – An acronym that stands for Long-term Equity Anticipation Securities. About 40% of the optionable stocks available, they are traded under different root symbols than the normal option series and only expire in January of the next two years. LEAPs is a registered trademark of the CBOE.

Limit Order – A type of order that is placed with the broker where the investor can set what price they would like to receive for selling or buying an equity or option. It is recommended to use a limit order when entering Iron Condor positions so the investor can hopefully receive a slightly higher premium than the offered aggregate bid price.

Liquidation Value – The value of an equity, option or combination equity and option strategy if the position were closed. This can be expressed as a monetary value or as a percentage.

Liquidity – A term used to describe how often an equity or option is traded. For options, liquidity can be measured using the volume of the option or the open interest.

Long Position – When an investor is a holder of an equity or option position over a time when an increase in the price for the option or equity would be favorable. If an investor is long on a stock, they hope that the price goes up.

Long Call – A bullish strategy where the investor purchases a call option speculating on a rise in price of the underlying security, thus increasing the value of the purchased call.

Long Put – A bearish strategy where the investor purchases a put option speculating on a decrease in price of the underlying security, thus increasing the value of the purchased put.

Management Techniques – Methods that are used to help maximize the potential return or minimize the potential loss on an equity, option or combination equity and option position.

Margin Requirement – The amount of money an option seller is required to deposit or have available in their account to maintain and cover an option position. Margin requirements are set by each brokerage house separately.

Market Capitalization – The stock price multiplied by the number of shares outstanding. A commonly used measure of the size of a company since larger companies tend to have higher stock prices and a resultant higher number of stock splits.

Market Maker – An individual who sets the bid and ask prices for an equity or an option.

Market Order – A type of transaction order where the investor agrees to receive or pay the listed market price for an equity or option.

Maximum Potential Profit – The highest profit amount that can be made on an option position. For an Iron Condor trade, the maximum profit is equal to the premium received when the Iron Condor position is entered.

Maximum Potential Return – The highest return that can be made on an option position. For an Iron Condor trade, the maximum return is equal to:

$$\frac{\text{Intial Net Credit/Share * 100 Shares/Contract * \# Contracts}}{\text{Margin Requirement}}$$

Naked Call – A bearish strategy where the investor realizes a profit by making cash from selling (writing) a call without having the cash investment of owning the stock as in a covered call strategy. While the stock goes down, the investor keeps the premium on the sold call.

Naked Put – A bullish strategy where the investor realizes a profit by making cash from selling (writing) a put without having the cash investment of shorting the stock as in a covered put strategy. While the stock goes up, the investor keeps the premium on the sold put.

Net Credit – The total cash received for entering a position. For a Bull-Put Credit Spread, it is the price of the purchased put option subtracted from the price of the sold put option. For a Bear-Call Credit Spread, it is the price of the purchased call option subtracted from the price of the sold call option. For an Iron Condor, it is the sum price of the purchased put option subtracted from the price of the sold put option plus the price of the purchased call option subtracted from the price of the sold call option.

Neutral Sentiment – The sentiment that a stock or the market in general will remain in a sideways trading range over a period of time.

Open Interest – Open interest represents the number of open option contracts on the market over the life of the contract. The open interest is a measure of how liquid the option contracts can be. When there is little or no open interest for an option, it can still be liquid because the Options Clearing Corporation (OCC) will make a market for it.

Option – A derivative investment vehicle that is a contract to purchase or sell shares of the underlying stock. There are two types of options, calls and puts.

Option Chain – A tool that allows investors to view various data points for all call and put options that are available on an underlying equity.

Option Series – The available option expiration months that an investor can use to sell or buy options on a given equity. There are three option series: JAJO (January, April, July, October), MJSD (March, June, September, December), and FMAN (February, May, August, November). Every optionable stock will have the near and next month expiration available.

Option Symbol – An option symbol is comprised of three parts. The first one to three letters are the root symbol for the option. The second to last letter stands for the expiration month of the contract. The last letter in the symbol represents the strike price for the contract.

Option Volume – Option volume is the number of contracts traded on the current trading session or on the last trading day in the case of a holiday when the market is closed. Both buy orders and sell orders will cause this characteristic to increase.

Order Duration – A specification placed with your broker to cancel the trade or leave it open based on the time frame you selected. Some examples include day order, good 'till canceled, and immediate or cancel.

Order Type – A specification placed with your broker allowing an investor to select how they want the position to be filled. Some examples include market order and limit order.

Out-of-the-Money (OTM) – This phrase describes where the underlying stock price falls relative to the option strike price. For put options, it is when the price of the stock is higher than the strike price of the option. For call options, it is when the stock price is below the strike price of the option.

% Out-of-the-Money – This is where the underlying stock price falls relative to the option strike price, expressed as a percentage.

Paper Trade – A useful educational method an investor can use before placing any actual trades. Paper trading with tools such as the PowerOptions Portfolio will help investors gain confidence and understanding of the market before placing real trades.

PM Settlement – Options whose values are based on an index which is settled or determined based on the aggregate market closing price of each component of the index on options expiration day.

Premium – Another term for the price of the option.

Probability Above or Below – This is the theoretical chance that an option has of being assigned. Specifically the chance that the stock price will be above or below the strike of the option. This is commonly expressed as a percentage.

Probability Between – This is the theoretical chance that the underlying for an Iron Condor or Double Diagonal is between the short option strike prices of the positions at expiration.

Put Option – A contract that gives the owner the right, but not the obligation, to sell a stock at the strike price before the expiration date. One option contract gives the right to control 100 shares of stock until expiration, unless the contract otherwise specifies.

Rho – A measure of the sensitivity of an option's price to a change in interest rates.

Risk-Reward Chart – A graphical interpretation of the maximum profit and potential losses for a given investment strategy.

Risk-Reward Ratio – A ratio of the various risk, risk-aversion, and reward values for a given investment strategy.

Roll Down – The process of closing a current option position or letting it expire, then opening a new position at a lower strike price for the current expiration month or further out in time.

Roll Out – The process of closing a current option position or letting it expire, then opening a new position at the same strike, one expiration month or more out in time.

Roll Up – The process of closing a current option position or letting it expire, then opening a new position at a higher strike price for the current expiration month or further out in time.

Sell to Close or STC – A type of investment action where an investor will sell any long option contracts in order to cancel the fulfillment requirements or obligations.

Sell to Open or STO – A type of investment action where an investor will sell any option contracts in order to cancel the fulfillment requirements or obligations.

Seller – A seller (writer) of an equity or option contract.

Short Position – When an investor is a seller of an equity or option position over a time when a decrease in the price for the option or equity would be favorable. If an investor is short on a stock, they hope that the price goes down.

Simple Moving Average – Moving averages can be used to gauge the direction of price movement in any stock. They are typically measured in 20, 50, 100, 200 or 250 day ranges.

Stop Loss – A type of order that can be placed with a broker to help an investor manage their positions. A stop loss will trigger a closing action on the open position if a target price is encountered.

Strike Price – The price at which an option owner has the right, but not the obligation to deliver the underlying stock. For put sellers, this is the price at which the investor would have to purchase shares of stock of the option is assigned.

Technical Criteria – Stock analysis criteria that is based on the movements and trends of the stock and usually interpreted through charts.

Theoretical Value (Option) – The fair market value of an option determined using a theoretical calculation such as the Black-Scholes pricing model. By comparing the actual trading price of an option to its theoretical value, an investor can determine if the option is overvalued or undervalued.

Theta (Time Decay Factor) – The rate at which an option loses value as time passes. An option with a theta of $0.04 will lose $0.04 in value for each passing day. Therefore, if the option is worth $2.73 today, then tomorrow it will be worth $2.69, and the day after it will be worth $2.65.

Time Value or % Time Value – Every option premium is made up of some time value and some intrinsic value. From its creation date to its expiration date, an option's time value decays away and any value left is intrinsic value, which rises or falls with the price of the stock. The percent time value is the time value shown as a percent of the stock price.

Uncovered Position – An option position where stock has not been purchased or shorted to cover a sold call or a sold put. Uncovered positions are typically referred to as naked positions.

Underlying Security – The equity (either stock, index, or ETF) whose shares are represented by the option contract that has been sold or purchased.

Vega (Kappa) – The sensitivity of an option's theoretical value to a change in volatility. If an option has a Vega of $0.13, for each percentage point increase in volatility, the option will gain $0.13 in value. As an example, if the value of the option is $3.50 at a volatility of 30%, then it will have a theoretical value of $3.63 at a volatility of 31% and a value of $3.37 at a volatility of 29%.

Volatility – A statistical measure of the annual fluctuation of the underlying stock. The volatility is used in option pricing models to determine the fair value of an option. Generally, the higher an equity's volatility, the more inflated the underlying option bid prices will be. Volatility is one of the factors considered in the Black-Scholes theoretical option pricing model. Several time periods can be used to create this measure. The standard volatility that is shown on PowerOptions is the 50-day volatility.

Volume – The total number of shares traded on a stock or the total number of contracts traded on an option for a given day.

Write – Another term that is used to describe when an option is sold. Option sellers are also referred to as 'option writers'.

MICHAEL PHILLIPS

Mike Phillips is a five-year employee of Power Financial Group, Inc. He is involved in the support and development of PowerOptions, an award-winning Internet site for searching for stock option strategies and PowerOptionsApplied, an Internet site providing an option-trading newsletter.

Mike has been trading stocks and options for ten years and holds an MBA degree in Finance from Santa Clara University, and Bachelor and Master of Science degrees in electrical engineering from Texas A&M University and the University of Texas at Arlington, respectively.

He was involved in the development of software and semiconductors for electronic equipment for many years and has been involved as a key contributor in the development of several start-up companies. Mike leverages his engineering expertise and experience gained from the electronics industry and applies it to the analysis of investment in stocks, options, and futures.

ERNIE ZERENNER

During a 30-year career at Hewlett-Packard, Ernie Zerenner forged a trail of achievement. He developed four patents, delivered six well-received papers, received an international award for his invention of the Fused Silica Column, and had an impressive list of industry firsts, including the first microprocessor-driven instrument in the analytical industry.

During his tenure, Ernie continued his lifelong fascination with the stock market, building a successful portfolio. When retirement loomed, Ernie felt it was necessary to switch his investing philosophy from seeking capital gains to creating income from assets owned. So he turned to covered calls, an options trading strategy designed to generate consistent income.

Using a calculator and the financial pages, it took eight to ten hours to find good opportunities to trade this strategy. In an attempt to cut that time frame, Ernie and a colleague designed a program to scan the entire market and find the best covered calls. The time required to do the job dropped from eight hours to eight minutes. It was breakthrough technology that earned a patent, and was the basis for a website called PowerOpt.com that not only supports Ernie's covered call investments, it supports thousands of subscriber/investors in, at last count, 57 countries all over the world.

PowerOpt.com is still the largest subscription program of Power Financial Group, the trading company Ernie established in 1997. Today, he continues to innovate and seek ways to help investors grow through options trading.

In 2004, subscribers requested an advisory newsletter service and the PowerOptionsApplied.com web site was established for investors who wanted Ernie to share the best trades found with the PowerOpt. com tools. The PowerOptionsApplied service has several model port-folios that can be followed or auto-traded:

- Titanium: A conservative covered call newsletter based on stocks

- Palladium: A more aggressive covered call newsletter based on regular and inverse ETFs

- Optium: An aggressive iron condor newsletter based on indexes

- Chromium: A less aggressive iron condor newsletter based on indexes

Additionally, in 2008 the assets of RadioActiveTrading.com were acquired, which included several publications:

- "The Sketch," a white paper describing the advantages of insuring stock holdings with put options

- "The BluePrint," a methodology for learning how to earn income from an insured portfolio. Ten different methods are outlined for applying this strategy.

- "Fission," an investment advisory letter following the methods of the BluePrint.

In 2009, the BluePrint methodology was integrated into the portfolio management portions of PowerOptions. Today, Ernie continues to innovate and seek ways to aid investors with education and investing related to options trading.

TRADING RESOURCE GUIDE

RECOMMENDED READING

THE FOUR BIGGEST MISTAKES IN OPTION TRADING, 2ND EDITION

by Jay Kaeppel

With over 50,000 copies in print for the first edition, Kaeppel's insight has undoubtedly made its mark in the options world. Now, he strikes again with an updated and more comprehensive look at those pesky mistakes that traders continue to make in trading options. In easy-to-understand terms, he systematically breaks down each problem and offers concrete and practical solutions to overcome it in the future.

Item #4941403 • List Price: $19.95

BASIC OPTION VOLATILITY STRATEGIES: UNDERSTANDING POPULAR PRICING MODELS

by Sheldon Natenberg

Unlike price and time, volatility is the one element of the market that is virtually invisible to a trader. Thus, having accurate methods to assess this elusive aspect is critical to successful options trading. With advances in technology, options have swelled in popularity and traders have risked their fortunes without an easy-to-understand explanation of the important factors in separating profit from loss.

Now, presented with clear and understandable insight are option-trading strategies, formulas, and definitions. You'll feel as if the master of trading, Sheldon Natenberg, is right next to you, guiding you through this potentially complex world of options.

Item #6091437 • List Price: $39.95

MAKE MONEY TRADING: HOW TO BUILD A WINNING TRADING BUSINESS

by Jean Folger & Lee Leibfarth

Want to be your own boss? Live independently? Take a more active role in managing your money?

That's what a trading business can mean for you -- money, independence, and complete control over your finances. But without the proper education, about 90% of people will fail. That's why this book is essential to your trading success.

Item #5312378 • List Price: $29.95

OPTION TRADING TACTICS COURSE BOOK WITH DVD

by Oliver L. Velez

In this unique DVD/course book package, you'll learn Velez's secrets to enhancing your trading skills through options. It includes a full-length DVD of Velez's famed *Options Trading Seminar* and a corresponding course book to ensure you have all the tools necessary to make money with options.

Item #5440077 • List Price: $39.95

To get the current lowest price on any item listed
Go to www.traderslibrary.com

NAKED PUTS: POWER STRATEGIES FOR CONSISTENT PROFITS

by Ernie Zerenner and Michael Chupka

In the first book in the Power Options series, Ernie Zerenner and Michael Chupka take on the topic of naked puts. You may have heard rumors that trading naked puts is risky, but these two prove that the rumors are outdated and the reality is that naked puts have the same risk-reward tolerance as covered calls, one of the most conservative of trading strategies. The naked put position allows an investor to take advantage of a neutral to bullish market sentiment without actually buying shares of stock. With helpful tips on using Power Options software, you'll feel like you're getting a personal lesson from these experts.

Item #5501177 • List Price: $19.95

PROTECTIVE OPTION STRATEGIES: MARRIED PUTS AND COLLAR SPREADS

by Ernie Zerenner and Michael Chupka

"How many stock positions have you entered after meticulous analysis, only to have the stock move in the opposite direction that you anticipated?"

It has happened to every trader — "the stock that got away." Now you can prevent it from happening again. The secret to minimizing your risk and meeting your goals is the use of the protective strategies you will find in this easy-to-use guide. If you are looking for a way to increase gains by reducing risk in your stock portfolio, this book is a must read. Start reading now to unlock the power of these strategies — to protect your investments and generate income.

Item #5840849 • List Price: $19.95

This book, and other great products, are available at significantly discounted prices. They make great gifts for your customers, clients, and staff. For more information on these long-lasting, cost-effective premiums, please call (800) 272-2855, or email us at sales@traderslibrary.com.